# THE VISITOR'S GU
## NORMAND

## Visitor's Guide Series

This series of guide books gives, in each volume, the details and facts needed to make the most of a holiday in one of the tourist areas of Britain and Europe. Not only does the text describe the countryside, villages, and towns of each region, but there is also valuable information on where to go and what there is to see. Each book includes, where appropriate, stately homes, gardens and museums to visit, nature trails, archaeological sites, sporting events, steam railways, cycling, walking, sailing, fishing, country parks, useful addresses — everything to make your visit more worthwhile.

Other titles already published or planned include:
The Lake District (revised edition)
The Chilterns
The Cotswolds (revised edition)
North Wales
The Yorkshire Dales (revised edition)
Cornwall
Devon
East Anglia
Somerset and Dorset
Guernsey, Alderney and Sark
The Scottish Borders
    and Edinburgh
The Welsh Borders
Historic Places of Wales
The North York Moors, York and
    the Yorkshire Coast
Peak District (revised edition)
South and West Wales
Hampshire and the Isle of Wight
Kent
Sussex
Severn and Avon
Brittany (France)
Black Forest (W Germany)
The South of France
Tyrol (Austria)
Loire (France)
French Coast
Iceland
Florence and Tuscany (Italy)
Dordogne (revised edition)

## Key for Maps

| | |
|---|---|
| ◈• | Towns/Villages |
| ═══ | Mainroads |
| ⤳ | Rivers |
| 𝔐 | Museum/Art Gallery/Centre |
| 𝛑 | Archaeological Site |
| ⌐ | World War II military remains |
| † | World War II military cemetery |
| ⛪ | Ecclesiastical Building |
| 🏰 | Château |
| ⌂ | Building/ Country Park |
| Ⓩ | Zoo |
| ✳ | Other Place of Interest |
| 🦌 | Nature Reserve – Safari Park |

# The Visitors Guide to

# NORMANDY

## Martin Collins

HUNTER
PUBLISHING INC

British Library Cataloguing in Publication
Data

Collins, Martin, *1941-*
    The visitors guide to Normandy.
    1. Normandy (France) — Description and
    travel — Guide-books
    1. Title
    914.4'204838   DC611.N848

All the illustrations in this book have been
taken by the author.

Published by
Moorland Publishing Co Ltd,
8 Station Street,
Ashbourne, Derbyshire,
DE6 1DE England.
Tel: (0335) 44486

ISBN 0 86190 156 8 (paperback)
ISBN 0 86190 157 6 (hardback)

Published in the USA by
Hunter Publishing Inc,
300 Raritan Center Parkway,
CN94, Edison, NJ 08818

ISBN 0 935161 48 1 (paperback)

Printed in the UK by
Butler and Tanner Ltd,
Frome, Somerset.

# Contents

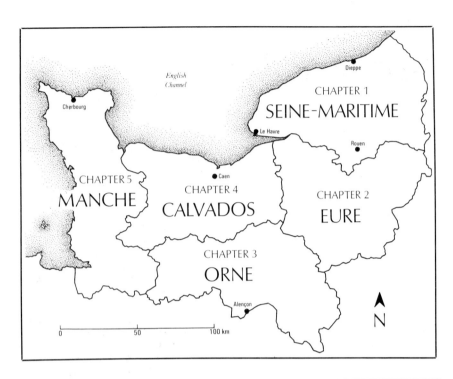

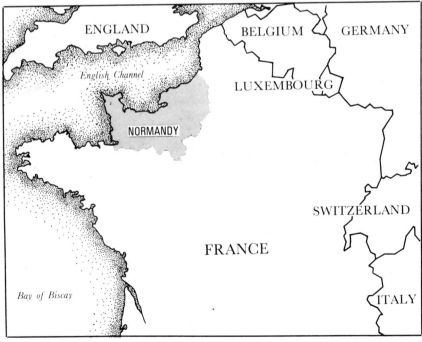

# Introduction

Normandy is a land of contrasts which offers much to attract the visitor.

Outside towns and cities, the countryside is organised in an unequivocally French style. Trees are pruned to the knuckle, decorating ridge and roadside with hypnotic symmetry; long, arrow-straight, big-dipper roads divide a generous landscape. In Normandy, the rurally quaint and picturesque — and there is much — can be admired with no qualms, since, on the whole, life on the land is free from hardship, however modest the enterprise.

Cities such as Caen, Rouen and Evreux, often fast-moving and busy, are softened by a consciousness of their own antiquity, an antiquity woven into the fabric of the province and around which so much of its attraction revolves. Indeed, an appreciation of its past, however summary, is essential to an understanding of present-day Normandy.

Under Julius Caesar, the Romans invaded what we know as Normandy fifty years before Christ (and were to enter Britain too, from the Channel coast). Normandy suffered further incursions by Saxon, Germanic and Nordic peoples up to the sixth century when it had become part of the Merovingian kingdom.

300 years were to pass, with major towns like Evreux, Coutances and Rouen becoming well established and the first monasteries being founded, before the Norsemen — those fierce Vikings from Denmark — swept south in the early ninth century. It was an invasion, a ravaging, of Christian Europe which left Normandy, and for that matter England too, a changed land.

Viking raids in the Seine valley, the Cotentin peninsula and eventually Paris continued for decades until their chieftain Rollo, and Charles the Simple, then King of France, concluded the Treaty of St Clair-sur-Epte in AD 911, installing Rollo as first Duke of Normandy and bringing a fitful peace.

Despite the consolidation of the new dukedom, the creation of monasteries and the restoration of the abbeys, the Viking temperament prevailed, with the 'Normans' continuing to raid and plunder as far afield as Constantinople, Italy and the Holy Land. Their conquest of Saxon England in 1066 under William, sixth Duke of Normandy, culminating in the Battle of Hastings, is one of English history's best known episodes and is magnificently depicted in the famous tapestry at Bayeux.

England and Normandy were united by a common leadership, and during the ensuing years of prosperity, great abbeys, churches and castles were erected in the robust Norman, or Romanesque, style of architecture originated by Benedictine monks. Many fine examples may be found in both countries, highlighting their shared heritage.

The Anglo-Normans, simultaneous Kings of England and Dukes of Normandy, quarrelled intermittently with their rival cousin overlords, the Kings of France, and when Château Gaillard and Rouen were taken from them in 1204, the Duchy of Normandy reverted to the French throne.

The Norman Charter, endowing full legal provincial status, was granted in 1315. It was not until 1450, however, three years before the end of the Hundred Years War which ravaged Normandy and saw it annexed again

*Allée Couverte – ancient burial-place near Cherbourg*

briefly to England, that the province was finally reunited with France, to share a common destiny throughout the Wars of Religion and the French Revolution.

Thanks, perhaps, to its restless and energetic Viking ancestry, Normandy's maritime fringe brought the province considerable distinction. In the eleventh century, the Hauteville family from the Cotentin peninsula conquered half of Italy, pushing on to Sicily and Greece before joining the First Crusade. Later, Norman adventurers reached to the edges of the known world — Brazil, the

Canary Islands, the mouth of the St Lawrence river, the sites of New York and Florida. The new territory of Canada was opened up by Jacques Cartier from Dieppe, and in 1608 Samuel Champlain from Honfleur founded Quebec.

In more recent times, war has engulfed this most fought-over corner of France. Normandy escaped the fighting of World War I which devastated neighbouring Picardy, but bore the brunt of some of World War II's bitterest combat, particularly following

*La Trinité and Duke William's Statue at Falaise*

the D-Day landings along the Calvados Coast on 6 June 1944.

It is difficult to invoke images capable of conveying the ferocity and scale of the conflict, especially in the *bocage* to the west. Whole towns were destroyed, and while brave and skilful reconstruction is to be celebrated, by the same token the loss of so much will be mourned for generations yet.

World War II is still a recent nightmare for Normandy and in waking from it she is not slow to draw a thankful breath. Commemorative museums, monuments and military cemeteries serve as a reminder of those tragic days, though for the observant

traveller the relics of war are all too evident, especially on the coast.

Miraculously, by no means all was lost and many smaller, non-strategic communities were spared the level of destruction that befell Le Havre and Caen. The wonder is not how much has gone, but how much remains.

Normandy's great abbeys and cathedrals speak eloquently of the spiritual and aesthetic foundation upon which a long and vigorous artistic tradition has been built. Honfleur and the Seine estuary were the cradle of Impressionism, Dieppe that of the later Impressionists and 'Fauves'. Many artists have worked in Normandy and

9

*Château Gaillard*

---

are well represented in art galleries at
Caen, Le Havre, Rouen and other cities,
among them Monet, Boudin, Sisley,
Pissaro, Dufy, Seurat, J.F. Millet and
Bonington. A memorial to the life and
work of Ferdnand Léger can be found
near Vimoutiers, while Claude Monet's
house and famous water-garden are
enshrined at Giverny.

Distinguished writers, too, have
emerged; none more so than Gustave
Flaubert from Rouen, creator in
*Madame Bovary* of one of classical
fiction's most memorable characters.
Also from Rouen came Pierre Corneille,
from Dieppe Guy de Maupassant, from
Caen the poet Malherbe and from the
Cotentin the eminent Barbey
d'Aurevilly.

A dozen great churches, some of the
finest in all France, vie for attention with
castles and manor houses, from Gisors
in the east to Mont-St-Michel in the
west. Religious, civil and military
buildings at all levels of importance are
prolific, and those in ruins are no less
worthy of a visit. Forearmed with a little

knowledge, imagination fills out the
story independently of language.

Frequently abbeys, churches, castles
and cathedrals adorn the very landscape
from which their stone was quarried.
The Seine's soft, chalky cliffs are echoed
in the buildings of nearby Rouen and the
great historical sites of the Seine valley,
while Caen's harder Oolitic limestone,
capable of holding more detail, pervades
the city and surrounding countryside. (It
was exported for use in England,
notably for Westminster Abbey, after
the Norman Conquest.)

Elsewhere, too, the relationship
between local materials and buildings is
clear to see. In pays de Caux, small flints
and stones from the plateau are locked
in copious mortar, while that ubiquitous
Norman resource, clay, is found almost
everywhere in the cobwork between
timbers, and as fired decorative
brickwork. Farther west, granite,
sandstone and slate conspire to subdue
the landscapes of the *bocage* and the
Cotentin.

Towards one extreme, Normandy's

*Eleventh-century church at Cerisy-la-Forêt*

domestic architecture is distinctively noble. High-sweeping slate roofs, with little upward flourishes like grace-notes along the eaves, end in great bluntly wedged gables. Façades are relieved by elegant archways and the insistent pattern of exposed timbers and chequered brickwork. The scale of farmhouse and outbuilding surprises: at times stately, occasionally monumental, almost always imposing.

But there is, too, a curious counterpoint; a rash of ruined barns, of patched-up sheds, pragmatically adapted and added to, symbols of an unchanging rural obtuseness. In many areas, corrugated iron has replaced the original thatch: its function, cheapness and convenience are easy qualities to appreciate, though its visual effects are rarely short of brutal!

In character with much of France, Normandy has its share of attractively eroded surfaces; old hand-painted advertisements for Martini and Pernod and Credit Lyonnais still occupy whole walls, untouched in decades. But it is the hypnotic grid of half-timbering which distinguishes the Norman façade. Often, in towns at least, the design is added, not

11

structural, with modern buildings paying lip-service to the traditional styles. At its most authentic, this conspicuous hallmark of the province can seem almost overwhelmingly picturesque.

Exceptions like Le Havre, St Lô or Cherbourg, rebuilt from the ruins of World War II, are reminders that architectural modernism is rarely a happy substitute for traditional forms and materials. The visual effect can be dehumanising and dreary, however worthy the intentions. Even so, such observations take no account of the inhabitants' spirit and it would be quite wrong to assume that such places lack soul or animation.

The Norman people, so far as it is ever possible to make generalisations, are not renowned for their effusiveness and can even seem a trifle dour to the stranger. Friendliness, however, is close beneath the surface, and since World War II the British, Americans and Canadians have been looked upon with special favour for the part they played in Normandy's liberation. The people of this green and pleasant land are hospitable and homely, industrious and proud of their flourishing province.

Normandy's is a heavily agricultural society for the most part, but the world changes swiftly and, in places off the beaten track, the methods of the small farmer can range from inefficient to archaic by modern standards. The land, it might seem, is worked by isolated figures in regulation blue overalls, *velos* (mopeds) parked on the verge far from the nearest village.

That, however, is only a fragment of the whole picture. On the Caux chalklands, powerful tractors plough arabesques on prairie-sized hillsides, while pastures everywhere support heavy populations of cattle: large-scale farming at its most efficient.

One in four of all French cows belongs to Normandy — $5\frac{1}{2}$ million of them! The distinctive brown-and-white breed, brought over from Scandinavia at the time of the Viking invasions in the eighth and ninth centuries, has endowed Normandy with a reputation for dairy foods of great quality. A good cow can yield up to 30 litres ($6\frac{1}{2}$ gallons) of cream-rich milk each day, forming the basis of an important cheese, butter and milk-product industry. Even in these

diet-conscious times, cream is still the mainstay of Norman cuisine.

Cheeses are legendary. Most famous of all, and imitated world-wide, is Camembert, made small and flat to ripen inside its penicillin-dusted crust in four weeks. Other cheeses include the pungent Livarot, Pont-l'Évêque from the Auge region, Cam, Boursin, Neufchâtel, not to mention the fresh Suisses, double creams and demi-sels from pays de Bray.

Normandy is a gastronomic paradise for lovers of French provincial cooking and seafood, with each region offering its own speciality. Thus one eats omelettes at Mont-St-Michel, white pudding in Avranches, chitterlings, pâtés and sausages in Vire, duck in Rouen, tripe in Caen and la Ferté-Macé, sole in Dieppe and chicken garnished with tiny onions in the Auge valley.

Shellfish abound: oysters from St Vaast-la-Hougue, cockles and shrimps from Honfleur, mussels from Villerville and Isigny, lobster from Barfleur and La Hague. Rich *sauce Normande* will accompany many dishes, as might *trou Normand,* a between-courses tot of the distilled apple brandy called Calvados.

Normandy has no vineyards, but *cidre* from its fine apple orchards is widely consumed and the fruit itself is often of excellent quality.

Horses are bred principally in the Cotentin peninsula and on pastures around Merlerault. Thoroughbreds, crossbreeds, Percherons, trotters and cobs are all represented, many in the national studs at St Lô and Le Haras du Pin. The sales of yearling racehorses at Deauville each August attract buyers from many countries.

Despite the importance to the Normandy economy of stock raising and small-farm husbandry (perhaps even because of it), there is no general tradition of sentimentality towards living creatures and it is always with a stab of distressed surprise that one encounters inconsiderate, heartless behaviour.

Farm dogs are often kept tightly leashed, rabbits, pigeons and other edible species confined to tiny boxes, live crabs' eyes plucked off to discourage escape on the quayside.

Such examples of callousness, common to many parts of mainland Europe, highlight the problems involved in reconciling expediency and tradition with emerging concepts of animal rights. For all that, they are no easier to accept. In a country whose religious conviction has covered the land with a forest of crucifixes and shrines, such contradictions are sharply drawn.

Industries based on old crafts still thrive in Normandy: copper-beating, weaving, reed instrument and lace making, pottery and wrought-ironwork, to name but a few. In season there is a proliferation of hand-crafted artefacts for sale on market stalls, quaysides and by the roadside, all exploiting regional motifs but subscribing as well to an almost universal European craft style.

Elsewhere, one is struck less by the factory here, the mill there, than by a concentration of activity in and around Normandy's great ports. Dieppe, Le Havre and Cherbourg together handle a third of France's maritime trade and are busy cross-channel ferry terminals too.

Like a sinuous artery connecting Paris with the sea, the mighty Seine allows ocean-going vessels access to Rouen, 80km upstream. Its estuary is flanked by heavy industries such as car assembly, shipyards and oil refineries; it is hard to overstate the river's importance as a natural resource and as a line of communication. Within its valley are also to be found some of Normandy's finest historic sites and many delightful riverside locations.

The diversity of Normandy's 600km of coastline is likely to surprise and please the visitor, for it provides such choice in coastal scenery and amenity. The north and east of the province were inundated by the sea around 6000 BC and vast deposits of chalk — ancient limestone from the ocean bed, hundreds of metres thick — were laid down and subsequently covered by wind-blown soil rich in organic debris. So the base for prosperous arable and dairy farming was assured, best seen in pays de Caux's expansive chalklands edged by exquisite white cliffs.

Farther west and south, rising to 417m above sea level in the Écouves Forest and the so-called Mancelles Alps, the Armorican Massif underpins the skin of pasture and forest with a ruggedness reminiscent of Brittany. The deep, wooded valleys of the Suisse Normande exemplify how these ancient sandstones, slates and granites, formed 350 million years ago during the Carboniferous Ages, have been split, creviced, reformed and eroded into a distinctive type of landscape.

Once again, however, it is where land meets sea that contrasts become most apparent: from the pebble banks and chalk cliffs of the Côte d'Albarte to dune-backed sandy beaches along the

*The Harbour, Barfleur*

*Needle rock and Porte d'Aval arch, Étretat*

Calvados Coast; from marshlands and river estuaries to high granite cliffs around the remote Nez de Jobourg.

No less varied are coastal settlements themselves. The bustle and clamour of large commercial ports is echoed on a more intimate scale in dozens of small harbours. Some, like Fécamp, Port-en-Bessin or St Vaast-la-Hougue, are important fishing centres and fascinating places to visit, with mooring facilities for pleasure craft. Major bathing resorts alternate with the modest and the positively sleepy! Whether your seaside needs are satisfied by the crush of fellow humans or by an opportunity to 'get away from it all' in quiet solitude, you are unlikely to be disappointed.

In springtime, blossom begins to push exuberantly from gnarled boughs and, at its first showing, apple trees appear to be covered by a false white frost. The four weeks of the *floréal* — 20 April to 19 May — are not always recognised by the weather, which will advance or retard blossoming at a whim. However, it is an extraordinary crescendo of prettiness, the stuff of calendars; Normandy in her party clothes. In fact, the apple crop is an important one, fruit being stored and sold according to variety, or made into cider.

Arable crops and grasslands occupy vast tracts of Normandy, but there are forests too, aristocratic stands of beech and oak and the communal huddle of conifers. They are well tended, their timber carefully harvested, and a delight to walk in, particularly during spring and autumn (though views are generally better in winter when trees are bare of leaves).

The French are devotees of

waymarked footpaths (*sentiers balisé*) and long-distance trails (*sentiers de grande randonnée*). Their broad and bountiful country is etched with walking routes to suit all inclinations, so it comes as no surprise to find them well established in Normandy.

On the whole, the terrain is easy, the weather moderate and the walking often accompanied by pleasant scenery, good food and much of historical interest. Longer distance through-routes do occur, as for example around Cap de la Hague, along the Côte d'Albarte and in the Parc Régional Normandie-Maine. The nature of the country, however, favours day-walking. Good centres are pays de Bray, the northern Cotentin, the Perche region, the Seine valley and the Suisse Normande.

Although Normandy is not, *prima facie*, given over to tourism in quite the same way as, say, the Mediterranean coast or pays de la Loire, it is prosperous enough to have established excellent provision for the visiting tourist. It is worth bearing in mind, however, that quite sizeable chunks of the province are intensively farmed, with correspondingly fewer amenities there.

The 'season' for visitors, governed by an intractable French reluctance to stagger holidays, remains doggedly short — from June to mid-September. Notwithstanding this, there are advantages in travelling early or late in the year and for visiting places off the beaten track where the authentic, more intimate face of Normandy awaits discovery.

Normandy's climate is, on the whole, gentle and agreeable. There is regular and adequate rainfall, heaviest in October, though the east is drier than the west. Sunshine hours are generous, particularly on the coast, and even if greater changeability exists inland, temperatures are pleasantly high in summer. Snow in any quantity is rare in a normal winter. Mists and sea fog can affect the coast and the Seine valley, but more characteristically the air is clean and invigorating, with exceptional clarity of light. An arm of the Gulf Stream washing the Cotentin peninsular endows those west-facing beaches with a little extra mildness.

For bureaucratic reasons, Normandy is divided into two regions. Haute Normandie contains the departments of Seine-Maritime and Eure and is centred on Rouen. Basse Normandie contains the departments of Orne, Calvados and Manche, centred on Caen. While these administrative boundaries do not always superimpose neatly on to the country's topography, the degree of coincidence is great enough for each department to be considered as a package of landscape, history and amenity, with just a little overlapping here and there.

Such a densely-settled region as Normandy will always hold a potential for the unpredictable that no guide, however comprehensive, can anticipate: the enduring experiences are, in any case, usually the personal and subjective ones. It is hoped, however, that this book, by providing background material and evoking the spirit of Normandy, will help the reader enjoy an informed and rewarding visit.

# 1 Seine - Maritime

The department of Seine-Maritime occupies a roughly triangular wedge of land with its apex at Le Havre in the west, its base running along the border with Picardy to the east.

In Rouen, and the great abbey ruins of the Seine valley, the province's illustrious past is powerfully and tangibly transmitted to the present day: history at its accessible best. The lower Seine, dredged and embanked to accommodate modern shipping, lies to the south of a vast chalk plateau given over to agriculture: pays de Caux. Its coastal frieze of chalk cliffs is encrusted with resorts and harbours, while inland, villages and half-timbered farmsteads punctuate fields of wheat, sugar-beet and flax. Further east stand the communal forests of Eawy and Eu and the water-meadows of pays de Bray, historically the larder of Paris, a green oasis amongst limestone hills.

The suggested itinerary starts from Le Havre, swinging clockwise round the department to end at the Seine estuary close to the starting point.

Le Havre was founded in 1509 by François I to replace a silting-up Harfleur (the original harbour); it is currently France's principal Atlantic port. Here, where the mouth of the Seine reaches a width of 9km, tides are swift, but a natural pause of up to two hours at high water favoured the new site and it developed rapidly. The port became a major centre for the importation of products from the French colonies — sugar, tobacco, exotic woods, coffee and textiles; a kind of French Liverpool. It also contributed significantly to France's commercial trade with North America.

During World War II, Le Havre's strategic position (Napoleon declared Le Havre, Rouen and Paris to be 'but a single town of which the Seine is the main street') brought devastation. The city suffered no less than 146 air raids and was virtually razed to the ground. Together, the French and the Allies laboured for more than two years to clear the debris so that reconstruction could begin. From being Europe's most severely bomb-damaged port, Le Havre rose like a phoenix from the ashes and at the present time is surpassed in importance only by Marseille.

Rebuilding of the war-ravaged city was orchestrated by a contemporary of le Corbusier; an urbanist and the pioneer of reinforced concrete called Auguste Perret. It is a most un-French place, a 'Legoland' of grey towers. On closer acquaintance, it appears homogeneous enough, yet is massively impersonal. Near the centre, one of Europe's largest city squares — Place de l'Hôtel-de-Ville — is surrounded by remote, inscrutable buildings.

At a time when tower blocks and civic monumentality seemed to herald an exciting jump forward in architectural design, Perret's Le Havre was hailed as the ideal twentieth-century town, a blueprint for the new modernism and construction techniques. Living units, it is true, were imaginatively integrated above shops and offices, streets given wide, airy perspectives, traffic and pedestrians allowed generous space. But the era of 'Big is Beautiful' is gone, and today's public is likely to level criticism rather than praise at the lack of human scale or intimacy.

While the motorist enjoys almost unlimited parking and free-flowing circulation of traffic, pedestrians often find shops too widely dispersed, the persistent repetition of the rectangular

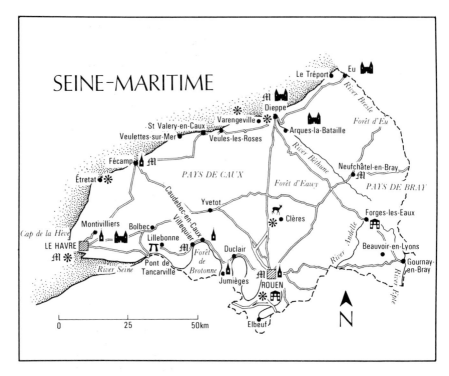

SEINE-MARITIME

grid unyielding and institutional.

For these very reasons, however, Le Havre is not without interest for the visitor. It is all worth a look, preferably on foot, and there are many good shops, hotels and restaurants. Leading out towards the sea, tree-lined Avenue Foch has been compared, charitably perhaps, with the Champs Elysées in Paris, while Perret's own Église St Joseph — a conspicuous and stark edifice 100m high — has an interesting interior on an unusual square plan.

On Le Havre's seafront stands the André Malraux Musée des Beaux Arts, an all-glass-and-metal structure with innovative roof lighting filtering through to multi-level galleries. It houses an important collection of works by Raoul Dufy (a native of the city), Corot, Renoir, Monet, Picasso, Sisley, Léger, Boudin, the Fauves and others. There are also tapestries, glass, pre-Columbian and Etruscan art.

In the St François quarter near the

Bassin du Commerce can be found a restored seventeenth-century house containing a museum of old Le Havre; exhibits include pottery, documents, model ships, engravings and Gallo-Roman glassware.

East beyond the Abbaye de Graville, with its little museum of tombstones, polychrome statues and model Norman houses, stands the original medieval port of Harfleur. It is almost lost amid a maze of new road flyovers and underpasses. Features of charm and character still exist, notably the slender, pale-grey fifteenth-century steeple of Église St Martin, but the effect of its remaining antiquity is dissipated by modern cubiform buildings and the heavily industrial hinterland.

To the north of the city, an impressive tunnel carries road, cycle track and pavement up to 700 acres of oak, beech and birch. Forêt de Montgeon is a modern amenity area with a boating lake, sportsfields, ice rink, an 18-hole

18

golf course and a large campsite. (Roads are one-way at weekends and public holidays.)

Le Havre does have a beach, albeit a pebbly one largely obscured by phalanxes of white wooden huts served by the occasional bar. It runs north from the marina at the end of Avenue Foch to the smart villas and picturesque cafés of Ste Addresse, from whose hilltop fort there is a magnificent panorama of city, port and estuary. On a clear day, the Calvados Coast is visible beyond the Côte de Grâce. There are good views, too, from the Digue Nord breakwater which helps protect the entrance to Le Havre and the yacht marina.

The old Bassin du Commerce, bisected by the Pont de la Bourse footbridge, is now used for pleasure craft, but elsewhere in Le Havre's busy maritime centre, large ships may be seen moored at quaysides or being manoeuvred through locks. There are 27km of docks around a complex of basins, and boat trips to view all this activity are available.

In addition to a prodigious tonnage of imports and exports (the major portion of which is petro-chemicals), the port also handles British cross-channel passengers. Understandably, the attractions of arrival or departure on holiday often outweigh those of Le Havre itself, so that it has never really established a reputation as a holiday destination in its own right.

Before taking leave of Le Havre, there are three local sights worthy of mention. At Montivilliers, 11km north, there is the eleventh and twelfth-century abbatial church of St Saviour, and a fine timber-vaulted cloister gallery in the one-time charnel-house at Brisegaret cemetery. The Terrasse d'Orcher can be visited near Gonfreville, east of Harfleur; here, a rectangular fortress stands 90m above the Seine on a wooded cliff terrace, overlooking the great petro-chemical and industrial complex and across to Honfleur. A little further afield is the Château de Filières at Gommerville, off the N15 to Bolbec. This moated sixteenth to eighteenth-century building in white Caen limestone is set in parkland designed by Le Nôtre and contains Oriental porcelain, wall hangings, prints by Fragonard and period furniture.

Le Havre is connected to Étretat by the pleasant Lézarde valley through Montivilliers, le Bec and Cuverville — a route worth taking since the D940 coast road is some 2km inland, the cliff edge rarely accessible.

South of Cap d'Antifer (lighthouse but very limited parking), the long piers of the Havre-Antifer port are clearly visible. Built just over a decade ago, it receives oil tankers of up to half a million tons, twice the size of the largest ships able to enter Le Havre itself.

Beautiful chalk cliffs, striated with flints and yellow marl, roll north-east from Étretat to Dieppe: this is the famous Côte d'Albarte (Alabaster Coast). The cliffs are sculpted clean and square by wave action, the sea at their base milky from chalk flints pounded on the beaches. At Cap de la Hève, west of Le Havre, erosion is sometimes as much as 2m a year, the former shoreline an

*City centre modernism, Le Havre*

underwater shelf 2km out to sea. All along this coast, beaches and small resorts occupy the outlets of river valleys between shoulders of vertical cliff, some reached from ancient hanging valleys — *valleuses* — left by the retreating coastline.

Étretat, of all the Côte d'Albarte resorts, is richly favoured and justifiably popular. Running back in a valley opening between the Aval (upstream) and Amont (downstream) cliffs, the little town is self-contained, with a sprinkle of charming features. In Place Maréchal-Foch there is a reconstructed, though authentic, old covered market hall (*Halle*) containing small shops. In the nave of Église Notre-Dame are incised pillars dating back, along with the Romanesque portal, to the eleventh century; the remainder of the building, including the lantern, is a century or so younger.

Étretat once attracted painters and writers, whose work was nourished and stimulated by the special clarity of light and the unrivalled coastal scenery. Guy de Maupassant lived here for many years. The cliffs rearing up to north and south are, indeed, remarkable: startling limestone walls, monumental pinnacles and arches, one collapsed to leave a needle rock 70m high. There are small inaccessible bays beneath the dizziest of drops.

Falaise d'Aval, reached up wooden steps at the promenade's west end and up a well-worn path, offers some of the best views. At the crest, directly above the Porte d'Aval arch (best seen from the main beach), stands an old World War II gun emplacement from which there is a magnificent view south-west to the Manneporte arch. A walk can be extended in this direction towards Cap d'Antifer and a return made by skirting the 18-hole golf course. Allow an hour for the round trip.

A slender spire atop Notre-Dame-de-la-Garde's chapel distinguishes the summit of the northern cliff, Falaise d'Amont. Shady steps lead between buildings, emerging at a steep, bee-line path to the cliff top. There are benches on the way for those needing a rest! The modernistic museum and nearby monument are dedicated to the memory of Charles Nungesser and François Coli, French aviators whose attempt to fly across the North Atlantic in 1927 ended in tragedy.

Views of Étretat from this high vantage point are extensive, and yet more of the coastline becomes visible from the crest of Falaise d'Amont, reached on a path from the chapel. The GR21 long-distance footpath to Dieppe also begins here, making its way first to Benouville and Valleuse du Curé, then linking all the small resorts along this stunning coast.

Étretat's beach is a grey shingle bank, scoured by storm waves into smooth steps. There is access at low tide beneath the beetling cliffs, but notices warn of the danger from stonefalls and unsafe wartime structures. A concrete seawall-promenade, up which local fishermen winch their colourful craft, is backed by a casino and glass-screened restaurants.

Times change, and Étretat's former gentility has been heavily overlaid by a veneer of twentieth-century facilities so that holidaymakers demanding discos, water-sports and ice-cream should not be disappointed. Even so, echoes of elegance and style linger on in this place so generously endowed with natural beauty.

Yport, a modest holiday centre a little way north-east along the scenic D11, has an uncharacteristically large beach at low tide, excellent for rock-pool fishing, and a small harbour protected by a jetty. Many activities are catered for, from water-sports to riding and walking.

With trawlers ranging as far afield as the Newfoundland Banks, and a tradition of fishing dating back to the sixth century, Fécamp is today France's principal cod-fishing port. Its economic stability depends upon associated industries — canning, fertiliser production, net and rope manufacture, cod-drying, ship repairs — and there are fewer concessions to tourism than one might expect. It has the unmistakable ethos of a working town: heavy traffic, a dearth of cafés and restaurants. Trawlers can be watched on Quai Sadi-Carnot in the Bassin Bérigny, while fresh herring and mackerel is landed from inshore trips on Quai de la Marne and Quai de Verdun. There is also a lively Port de Plaisance, and although scuba diving is popular in these clear waters, the beach itself is rather bleak and uninviting.

Fécamp, however, for all its gracelessness, is noted as the birthplace of Guy de Maupassant (he lived here for a time and used it as the setting for some of his stories), and as the home of Bénédictine liqueur. Distilled from aromatic herbs collected on the cliff tops, the first Bénédictine liqueur was produced here by Monk Vincelli in 1510. The recipe was subsequently lost during the Revolution, only to be unearthed again by Alexandre le Grand, whose name now appears on every bottle. A distillery and museum, with audio-visual shows, tastings and guided tours (English available), are housed in a vast nineteenth-century neo-Renaissance building in Rue Alexandre-le-Grand.

The great twelfth and thirteenth century abbey church of Ste Trinité is well worth visiting, as much as for what it contains as for its rather severe architecture. At 127m in length, it is one of France's biggest churches. Among many interesting features in the massively-vaulted Norman Gothic interior is the Sanctuary of the Precious Blood, which attracts huge numbers of pilgrims on the Tuesday and Thursday after Trinity Sunday. Legend has it that a mysterious boat bearing a few drops of Christ's blood in a lead container came ashore here in the first century. The relic is now kept in a marble tabernacle behind the high altar.

Until the advent of Mont-St-Michel, Fécamp Abbey was Normandy's leading

### Étretat
Sensational cliff path above natural arches and needle rock; extensive coastal views; pleasant seafront and town.

### Yport
Modest holiday centre with large beach, rock pools, water sports, riding and walking.

### Fécamp
Thirteenth-century abbey church of Ste Trinité; Museum and Distillery of Bénédictine liqueur.

### Les Petites and les Grandes Dalles
Tiny picturesque resorts in deep wooded combes.

### St Valery-en-Caux
More fine cliffs; Commonwealth War Cemetery.

### Veules-les-Roses
Family resort.

### Ste Marguerite
Colourful fishing boats, unspoilt Romanesque church.

### Varengeville-sur-Mer
Fascinating gardens; twelfth-century church and tomb of painter Georges Braque.

### Pourville-sur-Mer
Commemorative World War II museum with military vehicles.

---

popular and religious pilgrimage centre; the abbey remains are in Rue des Forts. Fécamp's Musée Municipal in Rue Legros contains ceramics, drawings and paintings, archaeological exhibits and aspects of life in pays de Caux.

The pretty Ganzeville river winds south-east inland, shadowed by the D28. Shortly before Benarville, the D11 leads to Angerville and Château Bailleul, a structure of surprising contrasts surrounded by parkland. Although the main façade is full of Renaissance elaboration, those at each side are uncompromisingly medieval, heavy and almost blind. Inside are seventeeth-century tapestries and much Renaissance furniture. Another worthwhile detour, due east of Fécamp, is the partly-ruined abbey and military château of Valmont.

Pays de Caux, a chalk plateau dominating much of Seine-Maritime, is farmland par excellence. Reminiscent of parts of south-east England, it is a rolling countryside of big fields, of woods on long, low ridges, of muddy tracks, farmsteads and small villages. Hardly the stuff of holidaymaking, yet in spring and summer, when fields are bleached by the chalky soil into variegated patchworks of colour and texture, the Caux is a visual delight, particularly south of a line from Bolbec to St Saëns, and east of the Varenne river.

Typically, half-timbered farmsteads appear as dark punctuations in acres of wheat, sugar-beet or flax. Most are protected from the wind by embankments of oak, beech and elm trees; elsewhere, trees grow on clay deposits and in copses on valley sides. It is a well-drained landscape, hence the need for water-towers, ponds and wells to sustain crops and livestock; monotonous, too, except where rivers running off to the coast or the Seine interrupt the scenery.

One such is the river Durdent, flowing down a broad, green valley from its source near the large agricultural market town of Yvetot, to enter the sea at Veulettes-sur-Mer. Yvetot was completely rebuilt after World War II and is known for a huge stained glass window by Max Ingrand in its Église St Pierre.

The tiny church at Barville, delightfully situated where a tributary meets the Durdent; the sixteenth-century church at Cany-Barville; and Château Cany (not open to the public) are all interesting focal points to take in within a pleasant region. Yet further inland, all to the west of Yvetot, may be found Autretot, an archetypal pays de Caux *village fleurie,* the Allouville-Bellefosse oak (*chêne*) — one of Europe's most ancient, with two chapels inside its hollow trunk — and the big country market at Fauville.

The Notre-Dame-du-Salut seamen's pilgrimage chapel and beacon, off the little D79, is an exceptionally fine viewpoint over Fécamp. Between here and Dieppe to the east is a string of little resorts, all variations on a theme of beach huts and breakwaters, chalk cliffs and pebble beaches, chalets and caravans.

Les Petites and les Grandes Dalles are especially picturesque, tucked down in deep wooded combes, not unlike those in North Devon. St Valery-en-Caux, an echo of Étretat, has its own Falaises d'Aval and d'Amont, both crowned with war memorials. It was here that the 51st Highland Division made its epic last stand in 1940, and many Highlanders are buried in the Commonwealth War Graves cemetery just outside the town.

Veules-les-Roses, a sleepy, sun-faded seafront between the ubiquitous limestone cliffs, stained hereabouts a delicate rust-brown, comes to life with families and children in the season. Sotterville-sur-Mer, St Aubin, Quiberville-Plage lead on to seafood stalls and high-prowed, colourful fishing boats at Ste Marguerite, a village with an unspoilt gem of a Romanesque church. Another unusually fine church, incorporating a wide variety of architectural styles, can be found at Bourg-Dun, 3km inland.

PLACES OF INTEREST IN PAYS DE CAUX

**Autretot**
Typical Pays de Caux *village fleurie*

**The Allouville-Bellefosse oak**
2 chapels in its ancient trunk.

**Arques-la-Bataille**
Marvellous ruined eleventh-century castle.

Walks, drives, old churches and manor-houses in the great beech forests of Eu and Eawy.

**Clères**
Château, zoo, wildlife park and impressive motor museum.

Varengeville-sur-Mer is an ill-defined settlement, scattered between woods and a few Norman farmhouses on the coast road. Take the D27 by a café, a twisting lane towards the cliff edge, to find the Parc Floralies des Moutiers. These remarkable gardens containing many flowering shrubs, rare plants and trees, surround a house built by Sir Edward Lutyens in 1898. They were designed by the English landscape gardener, Miss Jekyll, and are open to the public.

Farther along, at the lane end, stands a flint and brick church, mostly fourteenth century. Of special interest are many twelfth-century Romanesque features inside and the 'Tree of Jesse' window by Georges Braque, the cubist painter who died in 1963. His tomb lies in the cemetery, as do those of the musician Albert Roussel and the dramatist Georges de Porto-Riche.

An avenue of beeches just south of Varengeville leads to the Manoir d'Ango, a well-restored late Gothic complex erected in 1530 by Jehan Ango, shipbuilder and Governor of Dieppe. Steep-roofed and built of stone and flints around a central quadrangle, the façades are intricately geometric,

*Place du Puits-Salé, Dieppe's old town centre*

reaching almost oriental extravagance in the great domed dovecote. It is said there are nooks and crannies in the brickwork for 1600 pairs of doves! Though privately owned, the manor is open to the public.

In a field on the clifftops at Pourville-sur-Mer, a rather down-at-heel beach resort, brown and green military vehicles outside a war museum stand in mute testimony to Dieppe's role in World War II. On 19 August 1942, the first Allied reconnaisance landings in Europe, codenamed 'Operation Jubilee', took place along the shingle beaches from Berneval in the east to Ste Marguerite in the west. A thousand Canadian commandos and many supporting troops died on that fateful day, but lessons learned from this raid were to prove invaluable to the main Normandy landings two years later. No-one has forgotten the tragic loss of life, marked now by Canadian monuments and flags.

Originally colonised by the Vikings, Dieppe is France's oldest seaside resort and an unusual town in many respects. Its prosperity was founded on shipbuilding, its reputation on maritime

*Dieppe's town-centre dock*

adventure. In the sixteenth century, the wealthy and influential Jehan Ango, adviser and moneylender to King François I, fought and won an independent war with the King of Portugal. Not long after, Samuel Champlain set sail across the Atlantic and founded Quebec. Notable, too, were the exploits of the Florentine explorer Varrazano, discoverer of the 'Land of Angoulême' on America's east coast which would become the site of New York.

English naval bombardment in 1695 almost destroyed Dieppe. Much of the existing old town is eighteenth century, but some older fragments remain, including les Tourelles, a fourteenth-century harbour gateway now linking the new casino with a modern hotel! The great flint-and-sandstone walls of the Château are seventeenth century, the turrets medieval. Its interior museum displays Impressionist paintings, model ships and a fine collection of carved ivories from the 1600s when Dieppe was a centre for this craft.

More than half-a-million passengers each year, two-thirds of them British, arrive in Dieppe on cross-channel

*The great ruined eleventh-century castle at Arques-la-Bataille*

ferries. The ships dock alongside old houses in the heart of the town, dwarfing the port architecture. Trains run blatantly, if gingerly, through streets lined with arcaded shops, cafés and excellent fish restaurants, while the main shopping thoroughfare — the Grande Rue — is a mere stone's throw from the ferry terminal buildings. This lively, pedestrianised street is transformed into a vast, colourful open-air market every Saturday — one of the best in northern France. At its hub are the clock-towered Café des Tribunaux and the wrought-iron Puits-Salé well, both curiously Swiss in appearance.

200m away towards the harbour, near some of the best pedestrianised streets, stands the cathedral-like Église St Jacques, much painted by Pissarro in his time.

There are three components to Dieppe's lively waterfront. First the passenger Port de Voyageurs next to Quai Henri IV and the railway station. Next a Port de Pêche where catches of turbot, bass, sole and scallops (for which Dieppe is renowned) are landed and auctioned early in the morning. Lastly a Port de Commerce, handling Antilles bananas, fruit and early vegetables from Morocco and the Canaries, along with other cargoes.

High to the east and a prominent landmark, the fishermen's Chapelle Notre-Dame-de-Bon-Secours provides a superb vantage point back over the harbour complex and the Arques estuary.

Dieppe's 2km of mainly pebbly beach, the closest seaside to Paris and generally more crowded towards the west end, is backed by the Blvd Maréchal Foch, a broad, rather English esplanade flanked by lawns, gardens and sports amenities.

With many good shops, cafés, restaurants and hotels, a casino, modern night-life and surprisingly free-flowing traffic, Dieppe has much to recommend it.

Before visiting le Tréport on Normandy's coastal border with Picardy, a short excursion along the Arques valley will be richly rewarded. Arques-la-Bataille is a small industrial town famed for its ironsmiths, and named after the great battle of 1589 when 7,000 troops of the still-Protestant Henri IV of Navarre defeated the 30,000-strong army of the Catholic League; there is a commemorative obelisk on a mound above the river. Arques' real attraction, however, resides in the ruins of an imposing eleventh-century castle on a rocky hill overlooking the town. Built by the

Counts of Arques, it was acquired by Duke William six years before his conquest of England, and is one of Normandy's most interesting feudal remains. Despite crumbling, eroded masonry and encroaching vegetation, it is still a dignified and evocative structure.

Any restoration has been sensitive and unobtrusive. The keep seems untouched, all archways and mysterious cavities, history in suspension. From the ramparts path, outside a deep defensive ditch, close-up views are gained of massive walls, impregnable still, while below lies the Béthune valley near its confluence with the Arques, glimpsed through a frieze of trees. Access to the castle is steeply uphill from Place Desceliers in the upper town, or by a grassy scramble from the flanking D100 road.

Across the valley on a spur between the rivers Eaulne and Béthune stands the

---

PLACES OF INTEREST IN AND AROUND DIEPPE

**Château**
Seventeenth-century, with Impressionist paintings and carved ivories.

**Grande Rue**
Dieppe's main street.

Stroll along town-centre quaysides where cross-channel ferries dock and fish is landed.

Seafront lawns and pebble beach; fishermen's chapel on east cliffs for wide views.

**Le Tréport**
To the north, a lively resort and harbour with big Sunday market.

**Château d'Eu**
Near le Tréport.

(now sadly depleted) ancient Arques beech forest, only 6 or 7km from the sea. During World War II it was used to camouflage the launching of German flying bombs. There are pleasant walks here today, though the narrow forest roads are not all suitable for driving along. Martin-Église, on the forest edge, is well known for its trout fishing, while further upstream, at Varenne, there is more fishing and sailing on artificial stretches of water in the wide valley bottom.

The final reach of Normandy's coast from Dieppe to le Tréport, no longer the celebrated Côte d'Albarte but 30km or so of steep chalk cliffs delicately hued with intermingling creams, greens, pale browns and pinks, supports an unremarkable succession of hamlets and villages, not to mention the site of a nuclear power station. Long shingle beaches, sandy at low tide, stretch north to Criel-Plage, but cliff stonefall is a constant danger for the unwary, as is tidal stranding, especially at Mesnil-Val.

As often as not in season, le Tréport will be replete with Parisians, for whom it is an easy drive; they transform this modest fishing village into the liveliest of resorts. At times the atmosphere is almost fairground, especially on Sundays when quaysides become a colourful open-air market. There is a swimming pool on the front and many of the bars and seafood restaurants overlook the main harbour basin.

Le Tréport's houses, shops and restaurants utilise an astonishing range of building materials, from brick and timber to slate, concrete and flints, a textural feast which diverts one's attention from a paucity of stylistic cohesion. Old photographs depict a harbour in the days of sail little different from today's, though silting up of the river Bresle's mouth has progressively diminished the port's effectiveness. Adding nothing to the town's fortunes, a history of attack and destruction was compounded by the British who burned down Le Tréport repeatedly during the Hundred Years' War!

The sedate and upretentious town of Eu straddles the river Bresle just 4km from the sea. It is elegantly assembled around its splendidly-proportioned Gothic Église Notre-Dame-et-St Laurent O'Toole, after a primate of Ireland who died here and whose effigy can be found in the crypt. Built in the twelfth and thirteenth centuries, during the ascendancy of the Norman dukedom, the church was restored in the 1800s.

Much admired by Queen Victoria and the Prince Consort, and once a favourite residence of King Louis-Phillipe (1773-1850), Château d'Eu stands in parkland to the west of the town centre. It is seen behind a row of flagpoles, a large and plain edifice by Norman standards, dating back to 1578. Inside, however, it is beautifully furnished, with many relics of Louis-Phillipe and a wealth of portraits, wall-hangings and tapestries, ceramics, documents and glass.

The ancient forest to which Eu gives its name is one of three in Haute Normandie. It cloaks a plateau between the rivers Bresle and Yères, often 5 or 6km broad and extending 30km from Eu to Aumale. Once zealously guarded by the Dukes of Normandy, and later by the Counts of Eu and the Orleans family, it is now in the hands of the Forestry Administration who have provided many fine walks beneath a canopy of oak and beech. There are good views from the forest's western edge over the Yères valley around Poteau Catherine, above the village of Grandcourt. The whole area is scattered with numerous small settlements and unrestored churches.

Spread along an undulating crest of land between the trout-filled Varenne and Béthune rivers 25km to the south-west, lies another of Haute Normandie's great woodlands — the Forêt d'Eawy. It is crossed by many dirt forest rides and surfaced 'Routes Forestières', leading through majestic stands of straight-trunked beech, each tree a tall, soaring pillar of timber.

Eawy forest's centre around Carrefour-de-la-Heuze is best reached from the village of les Grandes Ventes to the north, taking the quiet D22 south-west, the D154 south, turning left to Carrefour-du-Châtelet and on south-east through dense forest. Alternatively, it is reached from Maucomble in the south, going north-west along the straight and hilly Allée des Limousins divide which crosses the D12.

The Forestry Administration, ever-keen to promote proper recreational use of their woods, have laid out picnic spots and waymarked trails. In addition, the area is peppered with delightful hamlets, old manor-houses and interesting churches.

We are at the geological edge of pays de Bray, a distinctive core to the Caux chalklands. The so-called 'Bray Buttonhole' is an eroded dome formed by the same contortions of the earth's crust which raised the Alps; it takes the form of an elongated NW-SE depression with a clearly defined rim whose south-west edge is cut by the outflowing Epte and Andelle rivers.

Encouraged by the presence of fertile soils, dairy farming prospered and with improved methods of transportation in the nineteenth century, pays de Bray became known as the 'larder of Paris'. Its economy is still predominantly dairy-based, though demand for its cider and dessert apples is increasing.

The transition from the bare, prairie-like Caux to the woodlands, meandering rivers and enclosed green fields of the Bray, often densely populated with cattle, can be dramatically sudden. There are several viewpoints which illustrate it well, including from the D12 above Bures-en-Bray, just north-east of the Forêt d'Eawy, and from the D77 between Londiniers and the Forêt de Nappes.

At the foot of the pays de Bray rim, on the Béthune river close to the Forêt du Hellet, stands the pleasant town of Neufchâtel-en-Bray. It is a major dairy farming centre and home of the famous cylindrical *bondon* which originally established the region's reputation for cheeses. The visitor will find a handful of picturesque old houses, an enormous, mostly Gothic church restored following war damage, and a new Civic Centre with a little theatre-in-the-round set amongst lawns. For displays of pays de Bray arts and crafts, including a cider-press, visit the Musée Mathon-Durand. The Béthune river provides angling and swimming, the D1314 north good scenery.

At Mesnières-en-Bray, a beautiful Renaissance château will transport the more suggestible visitor straight to the Loire valley. It is undoubtedly the Bray region's finest civic building and although now an ecclesiastical college (with guided visits by advance appointment only), a sight of it and the surrounding countryside should not be missed.

Forges-les-Eaux was once, as its name suggests, an iron-working centre, its furnaces fed with charcoal from the Bray forests. Today, an accommodating but unremarkable town, it attracts what attention it can as one of the nearest spas and health resorts to Paris. The eight curative mineral waters, taken in a small 'buvette' below the imposing casino and seventeenth-century façades at the spa-park's entrance, were popularised by Louis XIII and Cardinal Richelieu: they are immortalised there in massive

---

## PLACES OF INTEREST IN PAYS DE BRAY

**Neufchâtel-en-Bray**
Local arts and crafts, cider-press in museum.

**Forges-les-Eaux**
Spa-park with curative waters.

**Beauvoir-en-Lyons**
Good views of rolling Bray escarpment.

*Rouen from the Bonsecours Calvary*

bronzes.

The park and town offer more contemporary facilities for tennis, boating, swimming, riding and angling, and there is a market each Thursday. For lovers of the anachronistic, a Musée de l'Age d'Or is housed in an old bus near an incongruous turquoise fountain in the Parc de l'Hôtel de Ville. During the nineteenth century, Forges produced quality *faïence* pottery and a collection is displayed in the Hôtel de Ville.

Tucked into the far south-east corner of Seine-Maritime (and, like Forges-les-Eaux, a good touring centre for the region), Gournay-en-Bray is another big

dairy centre. It relieves the udders of local dairy herds of prodigious quantities of milk each day, much of it processed in the huge Gervais plant and transformed into double cream, demi-sel cheeses, Neufchâtel *bondons* and the Petit Suisse cheese for which Gournay is best known.

From the extraordinary painted-timber church steeple at Beauvoir-en-Lyons, surrounded with little balconies, it is said that Beauvais cathedral, 40km distant, can be seen on a clear day. This will be an uncommon sighting and closer at hand to this small hilltop village lies the rolling Bray escarpment. Scalped fields rise to heavy copses along the summits of rounded hills like nearby Mont Robert.

West of pays de Bray, uninterrupted farmland sweeps towards Rouen and the Seine. It is an evenly settled matrix of villages, hamlets and interconnecting roads, distinguishable in ways too small or too subtle for a guidebook to mention; but there is one surprise, as visitors to Clères will discover.

The town is shamelessly dedicated to tourism — a good place for children and a great Normandy attraction of its kind. There has been a zoo here since 1920 and today there is a remarkable wildlife park at the château, with free-roaming peacocks, storks, cranes, flamingoes, rare oriental ducks and geese, and many species of water fowl. On an islet in the grounds there are Indo-Chinese gibbons, and elsewhere deer, antelope, kangaroos and tropical aviaries.

Fifteenth to sixteenth century half-timbered houses, castle ruins and an old timber-covered market are all worth finding, while Clères' other *piece de resistance* can hardly be missed! Opposite the market, the vast Musée des Automobiles de Normandie contains everything from an 1878 steam fire-engine to aircraft, from pre-1900 bicycles to racing cars, military vehicles and seventy-five motor cars dating from 1895 to the present day.

Rouen is the pivot around which not just Seine-Maritime but the whole of Haute Normandie revolves. Perfectly located on the Seine, in a valley of wooded hills between Paris and the sea, it is a city of great antiquity and exuberance; any visit to Normandy would be incomplete without a visit to Rouen.

By way of introduction, take the N14 towards Pontoise, turning off right at Mt Thuringe hilltop above the city. In front of the nineteenth-century neo-Gothic Basilica of Bonsecours, a popular place of pilgrimage, there is a stone balcony surrounding an imposing Calvary. Views from here take in the river bend,

the industrial left bank, several bridges and, to the right over wooded hillside, the unmistakable green roofs of the Cathédrale Notre-Dame. (Another fine viewpoint is Côte Ste Catherine, a spur separating the Seine and Robec valleys.)

Rollo the Viking, first Duke of Normandy following the treaty of St Clair-sur-Epte in 911, was baptised at Rouen and began systematically improving the Seine's navigable channel and building bridges: work was to continue until the nineteenth century.

The city suffered badly during the Hundred Years' War and is perhaps best known as the place where Joan of Arc was burned at the stake by the English on 30 May 1431. As her ashes were thrown to the wind, they declared, 'We are lost: we have burned a saint'. A waxworks museum with books, manuscripts, posters and models illustrating her life, trial and execution can be found in Place du Vieux Marché.

All up Rue Jeanne d'Arc are fascinating narrow side streets, criss-crossed by pedestrianised alleys. At the northern end stands the charming railway station designed in 1928 by Adolphe Dervaux.

Despite war damage by fire in 1940 and by aerial bombardment in 1944, many of Rouen's important buildings were spared; those that were not have been lovingly restored, so that today the city bears the title *Ville Musée*. Fifteenth to seventeenth century houses on timber frames, which withstood the bombing well, are particularly in evidence around the cathedral, notably in Rue Damiette, Place Barthélémy, Rue St Romain, Rue de Carmes and Rue Beauvoisine. A town plan to help you explore may be obtained from the *Office de Tourisme* in Place de la Cathédrale.

Cathédrale Notre-Dame, right at the centre of *Vieux Rouen,* is one of France's most beautiful church buildings. Constructed between the twelfth and sixteenth centuries, the great pinnacled and ornamented façades, the disparate Tour de Beurre and Tour de St

Romanus, the marvellous doorways and windows, all surmounted by a central lantern tower and spire soaring to 151m, add up to a veritable lesson in the history of Gothic architecture.

Although a touch severe, the interior is little short of majestic. There is an exceptionally fine thirteenth-century choir, an eleventh-century circular crypt with its original altar and well, and cloisters containing recumbent effigies of, amongst others, Rollo, Richard the Lionheart and William Longsword. There are also five very beautiful thirteenth-century stained glass windows.

In common with much of Rouen, the cathedral was damaged during World War II. Restoration work has continued for over thirty years, specifically to the transept piers, the nave vaulting and side aisles, the Calende doorway and the cast-iron spire, highest in France and now reinforced with stainless steel.

Another gem of Flamboyant Gothic architecture just east of the Cathédrale in Place Barthélémy, Église St Maclou displays an impressive west façade with fine Renaissance carved panels in two of the doors. In adjoining Rue Martainville is the Aître St Maclou, a rare example of a medieval charnel-house or plague cemetery. Wooden galleries surround a central courtyard, while macabre motifs of skulls, bones and grave-diggers' tools decorate the ground floor columns, formerly door-frames. The complex is now an Art School.

Other worthwhile sights include the broad Renaissance façade of the Palais de Justice on Rue aux Juifs, floodlit at night; 100m south is the Rue du Gros-Horloge, with its cobblestones, cafés and shops beneath half-timbered dwellings — perhaps Rouen's most evocative corner and culminating in its most popular monument. The huge, ornate medieval clock can be visited, as can the Donjon in Rue Bouvreuil, last remains of the castle built by Phillipe Auguste in which Joan of Arc was held prisoner. An exhibition of her life has been set up there.

Museums abound in Rouen. Normandy's finest art gallery, the Musée des Beaux Arts in Square Verdrel, houses not only an outstanding collection of Rouen ceramics but also a large and comprehensive range of paintings by Dutch, Italian, Flemish and Spanish schools, as well as the French Impressionists from Renoir to Dufy. Represented here are Velasquez, Rubens, Poussin, Fragonard, Delacroix, Géricault, Monet, Corot and many others.

Tickets to the art gallery also cover entry to the inner workings of the Gros-Horloge, and to the Musée de Ferronnerie, a quite extraordinary accumulation of over 14,000 items of ironwork, from door knockers to balconies, domestic utensils to jewellery.

---

### PLACES OF INTEREST IN ROUEN

**Panoramas over Seine and city from Bonsecours Basilica and Côte Ste Catherine.**

**Waxworks museum to Joan of Arc.**

**Fascinating alleyways, pedestrianised streets and old houses; pavement cafés, markets, shops, street theatre.**

**Cathédrale Notre-Dame**
One of France's most beautiful church buildings.

Many fine civic and religious edifices, floodlit in season.

**Gros-Horloge**
Ornate medieval clock; visit the mechanism.

**Museums**
Fine Art, decorative ironwork, Rouen ceramics, Joan of Arc, playwright Pierre Corneille, writer Gustave Flaubert.

*Excercising racehorses, Deauville*

*Caen castle in springtime*

*Crasvillerie manor house,
near Barfleur*

*Cap Lévy, northern
Cotentin*

*Springtime on the Jumièges promontory*

Some exhibits are very old and of unique interest.

In Rue de la Pie stands the birthplace and house of playwright Pierre Corneille (1606-84), often considered the father of French classical tragedy. There are original editions of his books, and seventeenth-century furniture; further material may be found in the Manoire de Pierre-Corneille, 8km south on N138 at Petit Couronne.

The Musée de Flaubert et l'Histoire de la Médicine at 51 Rue de Lecat (the Hôtel-Dieu) occupies the original home of the Flauberts and exhibits books, furniture and effects belonging to the writer Gustave (1821-80), along with surgical instruments associated with his medical family.

Located in the cloister of a seventeenth-century convent, the Musée des Antiquités contains material from prehistory to the nineteenth century, including religious gold and silver plate and other detail, furniture and tapestries, enamels, fifth to sixteenth century icons and old carved Rouen façades. Also to be found there are Gallo-Roman bronzes, glassware, and the Lillebonne mosaic, a large illuminated manuscript depicting a deer hunt. There are paintings too, and a Musée d'Histoire Naturelle adjoins.

16km to the east of Rouen, at

Martainville on the N31, the Musée d'Art Populaire Normand is well worth visiting, not only for the exhibits — an illuminating glimpse of pre-1700 Norman rural life — but for the house also, a fifteenth-century brick-and-stone château with massive round towers and associated farm buildings.

Rouen is France's fourth largest port, after Marseille, Le Havre and Dunkerque. Ocean-going vessels are able to navigate the Seine on a flood tide

watch shipping activity. In the city itself there is all the animation and bustle one would expect from a major commercial and tourist centre: markets on most days of the week, a Sunday Antiques Fair, street theatre, pavement cafés, restaurants and hotels, all making it a very good place to stay in or to visit (though just a day will hardly do it justice!)

The statue of a nymph in a small wooded valley 2km west of the N71 Châtillon to Dijon road marks the rising of the Seine. It flows out from Bourgogne through Champagne-Ardennes and Ile de France to its mouth on the coast of Normandy, 776km away. A thoroughly Gallic river, vigorous and like a coiled serpent in its lower reaches, its role in the history of northern France is well documented.

Unstoppable Viking raids in the ninth century repeatedly plundered the wealthy Seine towns, its monasteries, abbeys and churches — until the spoils simply ran out. Rollo the Viking eventually conceded the lands his fellow countrymen had occupied when he was installed as first Duke of Normandy by King Charles the Simple of France after the treaty of 911. Viking descendants made good the havoc that had been wreaked, and by showing an innate propensity for organising and administration laid the foundations for a flourishing civilisation.

Subsequent history, however, did not leave the Seine valley unscathed. From commanding military defences atop crags on its many concave banks, to important road and rail bridges and heavy industry, the river has been of considerable strategic significance for centuries — a vital artery for transport and communications.

With one or two exceptions to the south, there is more to see on the Seine's north bank, particularly the *Route des Abbayes* to Le Havre. Before leaving the

as far upstream as Guillaume-le-Conquérant bridge, 86km from the sea. Many old bridges were destroyed in World War II and have since been replaced, but good walks may be found along busy quaysides on both banks to

vicinity of Rouen, however, take a look at the fortified Château de Robert-le-Diable (a fictional character probably based on Robert the Magnificent, William the Conqueror's father!) at Moulineaux. The feudal fortress may have been destroyed by the French in the fifteenth century to prevent its acquisition by the English, but even today's depleted remains are worth seeing. There is a waxworks museum of the Norsemen in the former dungeon, refreshments are available, and views from the towers are quite magnificent.

A short distance away to the east on D18 are the Roches d'Orival, a chalky crest reached by the waymarked *Sentier des Roches*. The steep path climbs past caves, runs beneath a cliff and rises to the grassy edge of the rock escarpment. It is an astonishingly pastoral place considering its proximity to the sprawling industrial town of Elbeuf, once a major centre for the textile industry.

By following signs for Lillebonne and passing Cantaleu, the small village of St Martin-de-Boscherville is reached. (A longer route ambles along a big loop in the Seine, through hamlets round the Forêt de Roumare. There is horse-riding at le Genetey, while at Sahurs there are good views across to Château de Robert-le-Diable on its wooded cliff.)

St Martin-de-Boscherville's abbey church of St George, dating back to 1080, became the parish church at the time of the Revolution and was saved from desecration. Ornamentation on the main door is typically Norman Romanesque, the Chapter House is twelfth century, and the whole building is well preserved.

A little way northwards on the escarpment near Henouville is a very fine vantage point and there is sailing from the river bank below. Further north still, Barentin is noted for its British-designed, 27-arch viaduct as well as streets filled with statues and other art works, including a Rodin sculpture.

Duclair is an agreeable sort of place, a waterside town of bars, benches and shady views of large ships plying the Seine. Duck is a local gastronomic speciality. A ferry runs to the south shore and there are moorings for yachts, as well as waymarked walks in the area. (The GR2 long-distance footpath from les Andelys to Le Havre follows the river bank in this section, wherever possible.)

At apple-blossom time during the *floréal* from mid-April to mid-May, the Jumièges promontory will provide the visitor with an unforgettable visual experience. A delightful little road, the D25, encircles this sheltered, south-facing teardrop of land, held within the last of the Seine's great 180° meanders, passing on its way endless orchards, vernacular buildings and farms selling fruit beneath low white cliffs. One senses open sea in the quality of air and reflected light: the estuary is only thirty flat kilometres from here and the broad, heavy waters of the Seine are always near at hand, gliding west.

Amongst trees near the small village of Jumièges stand the mellow grey ruins of the Abbaye de Jumièges, a site of outstanding beauty which some have compared to Fountains or Rievaulx abbeys in Yorkshire.

Founded in AD 604 by St Philibert, the original abbey was destroyed by Viking raids during the eighth and ninth centuries. Reconstruction began under Duke William Longsword around 925, though most of this vast building was erected under the auspices of a Benedictine abbot, Robert Champart, who later became known as Robert the Norman and was made Archbishop of Canterbury by Edward the Confessor in 1051.

A centre for scholarship and philanthropy, the abbey (at the time known as the Jumièges Almshouses) was consecrated in the presence of William the Conqueror in 1067 and flourished until the monks were dispersed during the French Revolution. A curious interlude followed, the abbey being purchased at auction in 1793 by a timber merchant, whose eye was shrewdly levelled on a ready-made source of stone for building! True to his purpose, he blew up the lantern tower and began the sacrilegious work of dismantling the edifice. Happily for posterity, a new owner acquired what was left in 1852, salvaging what he could, until the state stepped in and took it over for the nation in 1947.

Within the complex, a museum will be found in the beautiful Abbot's Lodge, which escaped the unfortunate sale and its consequences. There are good photogenic views of the abbey ruins, with their two impressive octagonal towers rising 43m on the west front, from steps to the right of the abbey gate. More distant views may be gained from the opposite bank of the Seine, to which a car ferry runs. Not surprisingly with such competition, the village of Jumièges itself seems unremarkable by comparison!

Across the river, and just in Seine-Maritime, is the nearest thing to wild country in this part of Normandy. This small forested wilderness of nearly 17,000 acres lies midway between the conurbations of Rouen and Le Havre, and forms part of the *Parc Naturel Régional de Brotonne*. Within this protected zone of beech, oak and pine, surprisingly dense in places, are many walking and riding trails, with only one or two roads intruding. There is a craft centre just north-west of Bourneville and a Museum of Ecology at le Trait to the north-east. Access to the area from the Seine's north bank is by way of the Pont de Brotonne toll bridge.

2km north of the D982, before it runs beneath the Pont de Brotonne, can be found the ruins of the Abbaye de St Wandrille. Founded in AD 649, its community of Benedictine monks fled from the invading Vikings and did not return until the tenth century. Their successors are still here, however, occupying the rebuilt cloisters.

Of the original abbey church, only two groups of pillars, once the opening of the north transept, remain standing. The cloister ruins are much more extensive and form a magnificent sight amid shady grounds. All four galleries, dating from the fourteenth and fifteenth centuries, are intact and bear several features of special interest, including a half-Gothic, half-Renaissance *lavabo* (washing-trough) near the ornate refectory door.

In 1969, the present monastic church, in the form of a fifteenth-century tithe barn, was moved here piece by piece from Neuville-du-Bosc, 50km away. It measures 48 x 16 x 12m; a massive, starkly simple structure, its great timber beams and supports all secured with wooden pegs. Inside, Gregorian Chant is kept alive and may be heard at Mass each morning and at afternoon Vespers. Relatively rare now in France, Gregorian Chant is sometimes encountered on recordings played over loudspeakers, as for example in the Abbaye de Ste Trinité, Fécamp.

Reached from the abbey by a path downhill on the right, past a sixteenth-century Entombement, round a small field and along the abbey wall, the tenth-century St Saturninus oratory is worth viewing. It stands at the edge of the old abbey porch and contains three apsidal chapels and some fascinating primitive carvings.

Striding over the Seine on slender concrete legs, its matrix of pale suspension cables almost fancifully modernistic, the Pont de Brotonne resembles a design drawing more than a feat of civil engineering. It spans 1280m, 50m above water level and was opened in 1977. After Rouen and the Pont de Tancarville, it is the lower Seine's third major crossing point.

Practically in its shadow, on a particularly lovely river bend, stands the erstwhile capital of pays de Caux, Caudebec-en-Caux. An attractively textured town, it was rebuilt like an amphitheatre after severe fire damage in 1940. Backed by hills facing across to the Forêt de Brotonne, the town and its broad riverside promenade lined with hotels and gardens is a thoroughly pleasant spot from which to view the busy river traffic.

Until engineering work on the Seine's banks blunted its effect, a bore (known in Normandy as *le mascaret*) surged upstream on big equinoctial tides, reaching spectacular proportions on the Caudebec bend. In 1843, Victor Hugo's daughter Leopoldine and her husband were caught in the path of a phenomenally high wave with only a rowing boat in which to negotiate it: they were both drowned. *Le mascaret* still passes Caudebec at certain times, but is now a mere shadow of its former self.

Caudebec's fine fifteenth-century Flamboyant Gothic Église Notre-Dame miraculously escaped war damage, though it is in need of some restoration. Its great 2,300-pipe organ, built in the reign of François I, is well-known internationally. Elsewhere in the church are sixteenth-century windows and rich wood and stone statues, some from Jumièges. Along with three adjacent old houses which include a rare thirteenth-century *Maison des Templiers* (now a museum of local history), this corner of the town has remained largely unchanged for centuries.

In woodland surrounding Caudebec there are several waymarked footpaths and sporting activities generally are well catered for: swimming and water sports, tennis, miniature golf and angling, amongst others. There are boat trips on the Seine too, and a ferry to the south bank. The Saturday market has been held on the same site since 1390.

Pilots of large ships bound upstream for Rouen embark at Villequier, taking over from estuary pilots. Villequier is a small historic settlement, nestling beneath the same wooded foothills as Caudebec. Victor Hugo's daughter and her husband are buried in the medieval church, which also contains some superb sixteenth-century stained glass. Not far away, a sizeable riverside museum dedicated to Victor Hugo displays letters, portraits, ornaments, furniture and effects associated with the writer and his family.

## PLACES OF INTEREST ALONG THE SEINE VALLEY

**Waxworks museum to the Norsemen, and good views from ruined Château de Robert-le-Diable.**

**Path to Roches d'Orival**
On chalk escarpment above river.

**Duclair**
Waterside town, views of shipping on Seine, local walks.

**Jumièges promontory**
Spectacular apple-blossom in springtime; imposing ruins of Jumièges abbey.

Walks, riding in Brotonne Forest, on Seine's south bank (ferries).

**St Wandrille Abbey**
Stately ruins and present monastic tithe-barn church; Gregorian Chant by monks.

**Pont de Brotonne and Pont de Tancarville**
Great suspension bridges.

**Caudebec-en-Caux**
Fifteenth-century Notre-Dame church and old buildings; boat trips on Seine.

**Villequier**
Victor Hugo Museum

**Lillebonne**
Roman amphitheatre and Gallo-Roman museum.

Lillebonne's second-century amphitheatre is one of northern France's most important Roman ruins; it could once hold an audience of 10,000 and is still used today for open-air performances. It stands right next to the D982 road, its grassy ledges and banks connected by crumbling sections of ancient masonry. Opposite, in the Hôtel de Ville, is a Gallo-Roman museum containing material which recalls Lillebonne's history. Indeed, much has changed. Following its use as a military camp during Julius Caesar's conquest of Gaul, this small industrial city became a major port of 25,000 inhabitants on the ancient Baie de Bolbec. It is now silted up and well inland.

These same alluvial deposits which choked Lillebonne and Harfleur are still accruing. Far from the threat to trade they once were, however, much of the lower Seine's vast industrial complex rests on this alluvial land, with room to spare for future expansion. There are oil refineries, cement and chemical plants, car assembly works, textiles, metallurgy and power stations — a landscape of factories, gleaming tanks, chimneys and gas flares.

Inauspicious though these surroundings may be to Tancarville, its elevation on the final wooded spur above the Seine sets it apart. Other than the great bridge there is not much to see. The Tour d'Aigle is all that is left of the tenth-century feudal castle built by Henry I of England; the ivy-clad modern château with good terrace views between high chalk outcrops is eighteenth-century.

Until July 1959, ferries were the only means of crossing the Seine downstream from Rouen. Today, the Pont de Tancarville, one of Europe's largest suspension bridges, saves motorists that 125km detour inland to reach western Normandy, with the newer Pont de Brotonne an additional option. Pont de Tancarville spans 1,410m — 608m between pylons — and for bridge enthusiasts there are telescopes and recorded commentary on the south bank (not always easy to find), with floodlighting at night.

20 industrial kilometres to the eastern outskirts of Le Havre complete the tour of Seine-Maritime, as well as providing an excellent entry to the north-west corner of the next department — Eure.

# 2 Eure

Eure is the second half of Haute Normandie. Its northern border with Seine-Maritime shadows the wandering Seine but in the east swings away to embrace the Lyons beech forest and the frontier lands of the Normandy Vexin, an extension of the Caux chalk plateau.

In addition to the Seine upstream of Rouen, still an imposing feature, other rivers and their tributaries flow across the department: the Risle, Eure, Andelle and Epte. As we shall see, their broad valleys hold much of historic and scenic interest, as well as forming divides between different types of landscape; vast open plains around le Neubourg

and Evreux give way to intimate orchards and crop-rotation farming in the west and to the great forests of pays d'Ouche in the south.

With a few exceptions like Bec-Hellouin abbey and Château Gaillard, Eure is relatively undiscovered by the tourist. It is full of visual delights — old towns, extensive woodland, a gentle and picturesque countryside which is quintessentially Norman.

By dividing the department, Eure's four principal rivers provide a natural framework on to which may be threaded details of the contents of each valley and its neighbouring areas. The starting

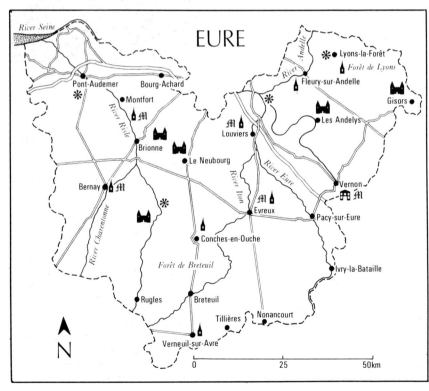

*A farmhouse deep in the Eure countryside*

point is on the Seine estuary at Eure's meagre 6.5km of coastline, first following the River Risle upstream as it curves south towards its source.

A wide, marshy bay near the mouth of the Seine, the Marais Vernier had seemed a likely proposition as good agricultural land when Henri IV first began a drainage programme in the early seventeenth century. He called on Dutch expertise for the work and it was they who built the Digue des Hollandais, the northern limit of the wetlands. Although 350 local landowners collaborated in the mid-1800s to extend the reclamation, it was subsequently abandoned until 1950, when a resurgence of interest promoted the excavation of 35km of canals draining into the Seine via the Grande Mare and Canal de St Aubin. Further reclamation and ditch-digging has involved clearing eighty acres of fossilised tree trunks — an embryonic coalfield. There are viewpoints at Ste Opportune-la-Mare and Phare de la Rogue, though today the Marais Vernier is a cultivated, rather featureless and often windy flatland, open to the distant industrial sprawl near Le Havre.

Pont-Audemer has been noted for its tanning trade since the Middle Ages and remains semi-industrial, a hybrid town of utility and picturesqueness. It sits astride two arms of the River Risle, linked by numerous little secret waterways, here and there like a scaled-down Venice. Good views may be gained from the Bras-sud bridge.

Though the town suffered badly in

1944, many half-timbered houses survived, some stone-façaded with wrought-iron balconies overhanging streets and flowery alleyways below — Cour Canel is a good location. One building of particular interest for its old Norman interior is the Auberge du Vieux Puits in Rue Notre-Dame-du-Pré, near the Bassin de Port.

Église St Ouen is worth looking at for its very fine Renaissance stained glass and some modern windows by Max Ingrand. A curious miscellany of exhibits greets visitors to the Musée Canal, including an important collection of over 10,000 insects!

The Risle valley is wide, its flanks well wooded as it penetrates inland to split the Lieuvin and Roumois regions from the expansive Neubourg plain to the east. Small settlements follow one another, many with a point or two of note, like Corneville-sur-Risle with its twelve-bell carillon in the Hôtel de Cloches, Appeville-Annebault's interesting sixteenth-century church,

and Montfort-sur-Risle nestling at the edge of the Forêt de Montfort.

Bourg-Achard, due east of Pont-Audemer, should not be missed by those who enjoy visiting old towns. There are many pleasant buildings of character off its broad main street, as well as a late medieval church with some beautiful sixteenth-century stained glass and ornate carved choir stalls.

It has been said that le Bec-Hellouin, a secluded monastic community on a tributary stream of the Risle, became the cradle of Anglo-Norman culture and religious development during the eleventh century. It produced, in Anselm and Lanfranc, two great Archbishops of Canterbury; no less than three Bishops of Rochester (one of whom was to become architect of the Tower of London); as well as many popes, counsellors to royalty and scholars whose influence lives on in institutions throughout Europe. The close ties between Bec and England are exemplified in the name given to

---

## PLACES OF INTEREST IN THE RISLE VALLEY

### Pont-Audemer
Picturesque waterways, half-timbered town houses (especially Auberge du Vieux Puits), Renaissance and modern stained-glass in St Ouen church.

### Le Bec-Hellouin
Magnificent abbey ruins and rebuilt monastery, museum and pottery. Vintage Car Museum off adjacent village square.

### Sentier du Vieux Château
Path to ruined twelfth-century castle at Brionne.

### Detours east
To see impressive Château d'Harcourt with period interior and surrounding arboretum; Champ-de-Bataille — stately mansion set in deer forest and containing paintings, sculptures, tapestries; events in grounds.

### Grosley-sur-Risle
Amusement Park and water-sports.

### Bernay
Ancient town with abbey, Notre-Dame-de-la-Couture Basilica. Museum and hillside walk in beech trees. Wild bird sanctuary just to north.

### Beaumesnil
Magnificent moated Louis XIII château.

London's Tooting Bec district.

Magnificent though the present-day buildings are, they result not, alas, from an unblemished history but from the major restoration effort of 1948-59 by the French Ministry of Education and the Department of Historic Monuments: together they resurrected both the fabric and the intellectual/religious life of le Bec-Hellouin. Their achievement will be appreciated when it is known that only the massive Tour St Nicolas and some outbuildings survived a terrible fire in 1150 which almost completely destroyed the original abbey, not to mention the Revolution purge which demolished the rebuilt version erected over the ruins.

Today, you can stand inside the tower and gaze up a dizzy height to the remains of floor timbers far above (the spire has long since disappeared), or climb 201 steps to the top for views of the Bec valley and the entire site, including a new abbey. A plaque explains le Bec-Hellouin's shared history with England in the eleventh and twelfth centuries, there is a small museum, and the monks run a pottery whose proceeds go into restoration funds.

The whole village complex outside is popular with visitors and justifiably so, for adjacent to the abbey is a Vintage Car Museum (Musée des Vieilles Voitures), holding fifty or so examples from 1920 to the present, all in working order. The little unspoilt village square, with its half-timbered houses and a créperie, manages to accommodate the weekend and holiday crowds with aplomb, and there is a Friday market.

By taking the *Sentier du Vieux Château* off Rue des Canadiens in the attractive town of Brionne, 7km farther up the Risle valley the remains of an early twelfth-century castle can be reached. From its square Norman keep (*donjon*) are pleasing views over the town and neighbourhood, as there are from the tower of the fifteenth-century Église St Martin.

*Château de Champ-de-Bataille*

Before proceeding upstream again to approach the forests of pays d'Ouche, a detour should be made east up on to the Neubourg plain to see the châteaux of Harcourt and Champ-de-Bataille. Scenery hereabouts is supremely rustic, providing a succession of cameos that are almost clichés of the simple country life: ancient barns surrounded by cattle and apple orchards, watched over by rosy-faced peasants outside low, half-timbered farmhouses. The *Route Vert* on D39 from le Bec-Hellouin through St Martin-du-Parc and la Neuville-du-Bosc (whence came St Wandrille's tithe-barn abbey church) epitomises this apparent Arcadia, and by taking any one of three minor roads south, the two châteaux may be reached.

Château d'Harcourt, a magnificent feudal fortress-castle dating from the late fourteenth century, has been owned by the French Academie d'Agriculture since 1828. Though somewhat tamed by seventeenth and eighteenth century modifications, it is still hugely impressive: a great, turreted, double-moated structure with a medieval gateway over the former drawbridge leading to an inner courtyard and a well 70m deep. On the ground floor is a period kitchen, while a grand seventeenth-century staircase climbs to Louis XIV furnished first-floor rooms. During the year, various exhibitions are staged, both inside and in the grounds. For good views of the keep and the contrasting towers, walk round the outer moat, which is 20m wide. The château is approached up a long, tree-lined avenue (some specimens are labelled) and stands amidst one of France's best arboretums, well worth a visit in its own right.

Arranged regally alongside a country lane off the D39 le Neubourg road, Château de Champ-de-Bataille is seen behind ornate but sturdy walls, a confection of pale, rose-coloured brickwork and stone beneath extraordinary domed slate roofs. It is one of Normandy's stateliest mansions, still owned by the Harcourt family who built it between 1696 and 1702, and is said to stand on the site of a battle fought by William Longsword with Rolfe, Count of the Cotentin.

Today it lies in deer forest on the wooded northern section of the Neubourg plain. Two low wings, each 85m long, are connected by balustraded arms to form a courtyard in which is set a white, domed pavilion. From the south gate there is a good view through the opposite archway over leafy parkland. Furnished with rare *objets d'art,* paintings by Fragonard, sculptures by Carpeaux, Canova and Pigalle, tapestries and historical souvenirs, the richly panelled interior with its period chimneypieces is no less impressive than the exterior. In addition, a variety of equestrian events are held in the grounds when, understandably, the château attracts many visitors. Other interests are also catered for with a golf school, putting green, bowls and croquet lawns and carriage trips.

The nearby hamlet of Ecaquelon, prettily situated in deep woodland, has a church containing some very fine sixteenth-century wood carving and an alabaster altarpiece brought over from England in the fifteenth century.

More lush countryside embraces Beaumont-le-Roger, and for such a small settlement — its population numbers only 2,900 — the Église St Nicolas is a bulky edifice indeed. Built on a hillside beneath the former thirteenth-century priory of Ste Trinité, it dates back 600 years but was badly damaged in World War II. Like the priory ruins close to a cliff by the road, its restoration is recent, with modern windows unfortunately having to replace the beautiful originals. The wooden figure on the clock tower is a Roman soldier — Regulus — who has nodded his head to the clock chimes since he was installed in 1826! For those seeking more active diversions in this area, there are water sports, mini-golf, an amusement park and restaurant at Grosley-sur-Risle, 5km south.

Following the River Charentonne upstream from its confluence with the Risle at Serquigny, the D24 and D33 roads are worth exploring as far as Anciens for riverside scenery and a glimpse of several fortified mansions and good country churches. The Charentonne valley is a centre for medieval guilds, still active, known as Brotherhoods of Charity, whose banners are displayed in local churches, the oldest at Menneval. A procession is held each Easter Monday.

Bernay is the largest town encountered; though of no great size it is typically Norman in character. The Norman Romanesque abbey next to the Hôtel de Ville was founded in 1013 by Judith, grandmother of William the Conqueror, and has recently been very well restored. Église Ste Croix contains a number of valuable relics from the Abbaye de Bec-Hellouin, but it is Notre-Dame-de-la-Couture's Basilica and its sixteenth-century statue of the Virgin (replacing a much older one) which draws crowds of pilgrims each Whit Monday.

Elsewhere may be found several old half-timbered houses, while more of Bernay's history is revealed in the Musée de la Charette in the seventeenth-century Abbot's Lodge near the Hôtel de Ville and Jardin Public. There is a charming little painting by Bonnington, a collection of Rouen china and items of Norman furniture.

Promenade des Monts, a splendid avenue of beech trees, runs along a hillside north of the town centre, affording good views over this part of the Charentonne valley. Just to the north lies the Parc Ornithologique de la Société des Oiseaux, a sanctuary for the protection and breeding of threatened birds.

Broglie is in pays d'Ouche, a less cultivated, more subdued region of scattered woods and forest on poorer soil. Quarrying for building materials was once a thriving industry, as were hundreds of local forges which have since been superseded by large metal-working factories in towns around Eure's border with the department of Orne, towns like Rugles, St Sulpice-sur-Risle and Bonneville-sur-Iton.

Broglie's large seventeenth-century château was the home of the Princes of Broglie, one of whom, Louis, won a Nobel Prize in 1929. Église St Martin is a curious mix of limestone and sandstone and the whole riverside village stands close to the edge of the Bois de Broglie commune woods.

Only the tower foundations of the medieval château fort at Beaumesnil remain; the present building, almost midway between Bernay and Conches-en-Ouche, was started in 1633 and took a full seven years to complete. It is reckoned to be one of the finest examples of Louis XIII architecture in the whole of France, an extravagant, richly ornamented façade watching its own flawless reflection in the waters of a broad moat.

Unfortunately, the buildings are not open to the public, though surrounding parkland is (except during August!), allowing visitors ample opportunity to admire the remarkable exterior.

A good centre for exploring this region and the lower Seine, le Neubourg is distinguished by a truly gigantic, square, sixteenth-century church with odd towers, and by some interesting old houses. All around, water-towers punctuate the vast flatness of the plain like white beacons. Roads, straight as ruled lines, radiate from le Neubourg itself, crossing thousands of acres of corn and wheat, south to Evreux and St André.

Though superficially less attractive than the Caux chalklands north of the Seine, this apparently monotonous landscape, created by large scale farming, is studded with timeless hamlets and villages, each with its conspicuous church guarded by a yew tree (considered in the Middle Ages to be a symbol of sadness and grief, perhaps because their berries are poisonous).

*Église Ste Foy,*
*Conches-en-Ouche*

Clusters of picturesque dwellings and orchards, with their complement of sheep or cows, characterise these settlements. There are castles too, in addition to those already mentioned: Château Tilly at Boissy-le-Châtel on D124 east of Montfort-sur-Risle, and Château du Tremblay-Omonville, just south of le Neubourg.

Its ring-road spares Conches-en-Ouche from heavy through traffic so that its delightful narrow streets, full of dark timbered medieval buildings and unexpected views, are pleasantly bustling with shoppers and sightseers.

Despite being a scant 18km from the city of Evreux, Conches emerged almost unscathed from World War II and has retained all the original character and charm of a hilltop Norman market town. It sits atop a spur between the forests of Conches and Evreux and a stroll on the south terrace opens up pastoral vistas of the peaceful Rouloir valley.

By passing through the Gothic Hôtel-de-Ville gateway to the Jardin Public, one confronts the ivy-clad ruin of a

twelfth-century castle — a small motte and bailey with several dilapidated towers surrounded by a wide moat.

Conches' elegant Gothic Église Ste Foy, built by a Roger de Tosney in the early eleventh century, contains some of the finest sixteenth-century stained glass ever made, as well as a modern tapestry of 'Christ in Majesty' (reminiscent of Graham Sutherland's piece in Coventry Cathedral) and two fifteenth-century English carved alabaster triptychs at the end of the north and south aisles.

By contrast, game and sports enthusiasts will find a complex offering a shooting range, archery, pony rides, mini-golf and much else, including refreshments, on the D140 to Bernay at La Ferrière-sur-Risle.

14km to the south, Breteuil is all but encircled by a loop in the River Iton, forming a lake around which attractive public gardens are arranged on the site of an ancient fort. Église St Sulpice is worth a look for its fine lantern tower and nave, parts of which date back to William the Conqueror. There are pretty waterways and the ornate Hôtel-de-Ville

*Waterway at Breteuil-sur-Iton*

seems almost miniature in scale compared to other buildings.

The English King Henry I designed Verneuil-sur-Avre to link with the other Franco-Norman frontier fortifications of Nonancourt and Tillières (now sadly in ruins), in a great river-based defensive line against the French in the early twelfth century. The town suffered badly during the Hundred Years' War, yet despite Charles VII of France's fierce, though unsuccessful, attack with a Franco-Scots army in 1424, twenty-five years were to elapse before it finally fell to the French.

Verneuil's main market square is dominated by the tiered and slightly canted tower of Ste Madeleine, standing away from the church and bringing to mind the Butter Tower of Rouen's Cathédrale Notre-Dame. Embellished in every style from Romanesque to Flamboyant and Renaissance, it is an architectural gem. Various materials used in the repeated reconstructions it has undergone are clearly visible, and the church contains some interesting statues. There are many good shops and hotels in the vicinity.

Built of red agglomerate stone in the twelfth century, Verneuil's Église Notre-Dame possesses a remarkable collection of early sixteenth-century statues, mostly by local sculptors. To the east, in

PLACES OF INTEREST IN VERNEUIL-
SUR-AVRE

**Ste Madeleine church**
An architectural gem.

**Notre-Dame church**
Local sixteenth-century statues.

**Tour Grise**
Views of town and surroundings
from this circular tower.

Ramparts walk and old buildings.

Place St Laurent, the circular redstone
Tour Grise provides panoramas over the
town and surroundings. Église St Jean,
to the north in Rue St Jean, is less
noteworthy, except perhaps for its partly
ruinous fifteenth-century tower and a
Gothic doorway.

Rue de la Madeleine, Rue Gambetta
and Rue Notre-Dame are Verneuil's
main thoroughfares, with ancient houses
to be seen on the corner of Rue de la
Madeleine and Rue du Canon; also at 28
Rue des Tanneries and on the corner of
Rue Notre-Dame and Rue du Pont-aux-
Chèvres. A walk on the course of the old
ramparts starts in Boulevard Casati.

The next excursion into the
department of Eure follows the River
Eure itself, south-east from its
confluence with the Seine at Pont de
l'Arche on the edge of the coniferous
Forêt de Bord. There was a bridge over
the Seine here even before one had been
built at Rouen.

Its former great prosperity as a centre
for woollen textiles (now replaced by
modern light industries) is reflected in
Louviers' richly endowed Église Notre-
Dame. It is famous for sixteenth-century
Flamboyant Gothic ornamentation on
the south wall and porch: the delicate
tracery resembles silverware more than
stone in its detail. Crossed by
interconnecting fingers of the River
Eure, the pleasant town possesses some

good examples of half-timbered houses
and a fascinating fourteenth-century
Convent of Penitents, almost Italianate
in appearance, by the river in Rue de la
Poste. The Musée Municipal, adjacent to
a delightful Jardin Public, elucidates
Louviers' history through displays of
local costume, lace, furniture and
paintings. While in this area, visit nearby
Vironvay's isolated church for its
exceptional views of the Seine.

A good touring centre, with excellent
shops and hotels on tree-lined avenues,
Evreux is chief town and administrative
capital of Eure. It stands near the
eastern boundary of the fertile
Neubourg plain on the River Iton, a
tributary of the Eure, and is a major
agricultural market for the region. Even
in the fifth century, when the Vandals
rampaged through its streets, it was a
prosperous place with a history reaching
back to the time of the Gauls.

Like many Norman towns, its periods
of good fortune have been matched by
disasters, and up to the fourteenth
century it was the stage on which
successive conflicts were enacted
resulting in fire and destruction. During
World War II, German and Allied
bombing raids devastated whole tracts
of the city, so that modern rebuilding
had to accommodate settings for the
antiquities still left standing: on the
whole, the problem was solved with

PLACES OF INTEREST IN LOUVIERS

**Old half-timbered buildings.**

**Fourteenth-century Convent of
Penitents**
On the riverside.

**Museum**
Local costume, lace, furniture and
paintings.

**Vironvay**
Nearby settlement has an isolated
church with wide views over Seine.

commendable sensitivity.

Evreux's great Cathédrale Notre-
Dame imposes itself upon the city
centre, a superbly restored amalgam of
Romanesque, Flamboyant, Gothic and
Renaissance styles — full of French
architectural flavours at their most
piquant. Arches in the nave are all that is
left of the original church; it was
substantially reconstructed in the twelfth
century, with choir and chapels added in
the thirteenth and fourteenth centuries
respectively.

Removed for safe keeping during
World War II, the medieval stained glass
is now back *in situ,* in all its glory;
especially beautiful are the rose-
windows in the south transept. Other
notable features to look for are carved
capitals and choir-stalls, Renaissance
wood carving on screens and doors in
the radiating chapels, and an
outstanding eighteenth-century grille-
chancel.

Less grandiose but hardly less
interesting is the abbey-church of St
Taurin, to the west off Avenue
Maréchal-Foch. The thirteenth-century
tomb of St Taurinus is a masterpiece of
the French goldsmith's art, and there are
several amusing misericords, in addition
to more very good stained glass.

A Musée Municipal of local history
and prehistory, including the Gallo-
Roman epoch, can be found inside the
*Ancien Évêché* (former Bishopric) across
lawns outside the cathedral. Promenade

des Remparts, alongside the River Iton,
passes the Tour de l'Horloge, a fifteenth-
century belfry tower, while to the south
of the old town there is a particularly
pleasant Jardin Public with trees and a
rose garden.

The Neubourg plateau continues
south with a regular scattering of
villages comparable to the country
described around Conches-en-Ouche;
many are worthy of driving through if
not actually stopping at. Larger
settlements like Damville, St André-de-
l'Eure and Nonancourt, more modestly
endowed than the better known places
with historic, scenic or amenity value,
are, however, equally representative of
life in this corner of Normandy.

From Nonancourt, Eure's border with
the capital department of Ile de France
runs east to meet the River Eure at the
village of Montreuil, thereafter
following the river itself for 20km. Ezy-
sur-Eure, the first place of any size
downstream and rather strung out and
ragged, is noted for the manufacture of
combs, once made from animal horn,
and for the nearby Château d'Anet.

Less than 4km beyond, however, lies
Ivry-la-Bataille, so named after a battle
fought between Henry IV of Navarre
and the army of the Catholic League in
1590. Henry's victory is commemorated,
rather obscurely, on the actual battle
site, 7km away near Couture-Boussey, a
village on the plateau famous for
making reed instruments. The obelisk
was installed in 1804 on the orders of
Napoleon.

After the battle, King Henry is
reputed to have spent the night at Ivry at
No 3, Rue de Garennes, a typical
Norman half-timbered dwelling. The
town also has a considerably restored
sixteenth-century church with a tower
and south door attributed to Philibert
Delorme, architect of the Tuileries
Gardens in Paris.

From the D71 on the secretive Eure's
west bank below the Forêt de Merey, the
brick-built sixteenth-century Château de
la Folletière may be seen between

Neuilly and the mills at Merey. Pacy-sur-Eure would be a useful base for a few days spent enjoying the Seine and Eure valleys; its Église St Aubin contains some splendid stone statues.

The D836 on both sides of Pacy offers fine pastoral scenery, passing through Cocherel, favourite village and last resting place of the statesman and advocate of peace, Aristide Briand. At Atheuil-Authouillet, cross the river and continue on the D71 for more delightful scenery before completing the round tour of the Eure valley and its environs.

A short but interesting stretch of the Seine crosses Eure from Pont de l'Arche near Rouen, south-east to Vernon. Its personality here is less maritime as it winds through undulating countryside, woods and villages pressing more frequently to its banks. In places, chalk cliffs not unlike those of the Côte d'Albarte are found along the waterline, elsewhere standing back from the river's present edge to remind us of its course in past eras. In fact, the Seine's serpentine meanders are explained by its extremely shallow gradient: from Vernon to the open sea — a distance of 100km as the crow flies — the vertical drop is only 16m.

At Amfreville-sous-les-Monts on the north bank east of Rouen, the Seine's principal water-flow control separates the canalised river from the tidal. Here, the Poses dam and big locks (*écluses*) regulate the volume of water passing downstream and enable large river barges to enter the tidal section. It is a fascinating place. A sensational footbridge leads out, first over the lock gates where long barges can be watched manoeuvring skilfully into the narrow chamber, then for another 300m across the Poses dam. Gaps in the timber planking caused by shrinkage reveal more of the Seine than some will find comfortable, and the heavy thunder of water passing through sluice gates just below can be felt through the entire structure. Turn right at the south bank for a view of the foaming turbulence, especially dramatic after a spell of wet weather. Back on the Amfreville side, a pleasant bar (*'l'Écluse'*) is open in season.

Appearing as a conical hill in the background, *Côte des Deux Amants* (Hill of the Two Lovers) is actually the precipitous lip of a plateau extending north-east towards the Forêt de Lyons. The hill was named after a legend — told in the twelfth century by France's first woman writer, Marie de France — in which Caliste, the King of Pitrois' daughter, was carried to the hilltop at a run by her suitor Raoul to test his strength in the eyes of her father: first he, then she, fell dead at the top and were buried where they lay.

The D20 climbs to a Touring Club de France viewing table at the summit. Another magnificent panorama of the Seine and Amfreville locks may be gained by taking a lane from le Plessis and following signs for Panorama des Deux Amants to the plateau edge.

Weather-sculpted white limestone bluffs and pinnacles along the Seine's

---

PLACES OF INTEREST ON THE SEINE UPSTREAM OF ROUEN

**Poses Dam and big locks**
Footbridge above river barges and sluice gates.

**Côte des Deux Amants**
Panoramic viewpoint.

**Château Gaillard**, les Andelys
Massive ruins above dizzy drops to Seine.

**Vernon**
Historic town; river islets, ancient buildings, riverside walks.

**Monet's house**
Studio and Water Garden of the famous Impressionist, enshrined at Giverny.

east bank are softened by sweet-scented hawthorn blossom in the spring; they continue past Muids almost to les Andelys. There is occasional access up paths on to the grassy escarpment, and some rock climbs, notably north of Connelles on D19.

Not to be missed by the visitor to Normandy, les Andelys and the great, dominating silhouette of Château Gaillard on its rocky spur constitute one of the most memorable sights on the Seine east of Rouen. Grand and Petit Andelys are twin towns strung together along the D125, their proximity to Paris betrayed in a perceptibly more cosmopolitan, urban ambience than villages and towns to the north. Buildings, however, are still charmingly half-timbered, many are medieval, and the main street is fringed with tall, tightly-pruned trees — that most evocative symbol of French townscapes.

Église Notre-Dame in Grand Andelys' Rue Général de Fontanges-de-Couzan dates from the mid-sixteenth-century late Gothic-Flamboyant period; it contains a Renaissance organ loft and some excellent stained glass in the south aisle. By contrast, the early thirteenth-century St Sauveur, in a square close to the river, is built on a simple Greek Cross plan in a much plainer Gothic style.

From the river frontage at Petit Andelys, with its pool and cafés, are views downstream of white cliffs and the diminutive Ile du Château: upstream, there is no avoiding the imposing bulk of Château Gaillard, to which all eyes are inexorably drawn.

This impressive edifice — the so-called 'Saucy Castle' — was put up by Richard Coeur de Lion to guard Normandy's eastern flank and deny the French king access to Rouen. Though apparently impregnable, surrounded as it is by dizzy drops, it did in fact fall at its first test, three years after Richard's death in 1199. Following a five-month seige, the French finally took possession and Normandy surrendered its independence.

The château's outer walls have mostly

*Château Gaillard from Petit Andeleys*

crumbled away, but the keep is reasonably intact, its foundations hewn into the very rock; walls are 5m thick and were originally three storeys high. A footbridge (the former drawbridge) spans the moat to the redoubt, only one of whose five towers remains standing.

A steep one-way system aids visiting traffic and there are superb views both from the car park (telescope) and from the cliff top beyond the château's perimeter wall. Entry tickets to the château also cover the Musée de Nicolas Poussin in Rue Ste Clotilde.

Château Gaillon, 12km south-west, was rebuilt by the Cardinal d'Amboise in the New Italian style, following an expedition to Italy at the end of the fifteenth century during which he was emissary of Louis XII; the building is said to represent the introduction of the Renaissance movement into Normandy. Also within the town of Gaillon, best explored on foot, are some good late-medieval houses, including a timber dwelling near the church and several Renaissance buildings.

The painter Claude Monet, leader of the Impressionist movement, lived at Giverny from 1883 to 1926 and is buried in the local church. His son donated the property to the Academie des Beaux-Arts at his own death in 1966 and extensive restoration work culminated in the inauguration of the Musée Claude Monet in 1980.

The intention, admirably realised, has been to re-create house, studio and gardens as they would have appeared in Monet's time. Visitors will find much that is familiar, and of interest, from precious Japanese engravings to the huge Nymphéas studio; from archways of climbing plants and flowering shrubs in the Clos Normand to the famous Water Garden formed by a tributary of the Epte, complete with its weeping willows, Japanese bridge, azaleas, wisterias and lily pond.

Close by across the Seine stands the riverside town of Vernon, a much-favoured place for relaxation for people as diverse as kings of the Middle Ages and twentieth-century Parisians who live only 80km away. Founded in the ninth century by Rollo the Viking, first Duke of Normandy, it is an historic town, though World War II left some of it in ruins. Old houses which survived may be found in Rue Carnot, Rue Potard and near Église Notre-Dame.

For an overall view of the town and several wooded islands, stand at the centre of the bridge connecting Vernon with its satellite, Vernonnet. From here, the stumps of timber piles which supported the twelfth-century bridge are visible, adjacent to the wooded ruins of Château des Tourelles built by the English King Henry I to defend it. On the south bank appears the much restored Tour des Archives, the keep of another fortress.

Vernon is a good touring centre, close enough to Paris for excursions to be made, yet with its fine riverside promenade and pleasant avenues, an attractive destination in its own right. Set in leafy parkland on its western outskirts, Château Bizy is a Classical country house from the mid-1700s with interesting mementoes of Napoleon and other military leaders on display inside.

The final section of Eure lies along and between the rivers Epte and Andelle, both hugging the department's border in this easternmost part of Normandy. This is the Normandy Vexin; historically a march — nervous frontier country hotly disputed by French and English kings. Forests are fewer, villages smaller, castles more prolific. Even today the open Vexin is less picturesque, lacking perhaps the humanising influence of myriad long-established rural communities. Shabbier than neighbouring regions, it is a utilitarian landscape in which the symmetry of man's planting is relieved only by the waywardness of nature's growth and the unpredictability of land forms.

The Epte valley to Gisors has played a vital role in Normandy's history. It was

*Medieval town of Gisors from its castle walls*

at St Clair-sur-Epte in 911 that Rollo the Viking and King Charles the Simple of France (a title meaning honest and sincere rather than feeble-minded!) created the Duchy of Normandy by mutual agreement. Towards the end of the eleventh century, this valley separating the Norman and French Vexins was to witness many fierce battles between the Kings of France and Dukes of Normandy. Ruins of the many fortifications are still in evidence, as, for

*The central keep. Château de Gisors*

**PLACES OF INTEREST IN EASTERN EURE**

**Gisors**
Mighty fortress-château, well preserved Prisoner's Tower with original oven, chimney and fourteenth- to fifteenth-century grafitti; medieval houses and riverside wash-house; twelfth-century St Gervais church.

**Lyons beech forest**
Criss-crossed by tracks and paths.

**Lyons-la-Forêt**
Delightful forest village, covered market, half-timbered houses, wooden statues in church.

**Abbaye de Mortemer**
Evocative abbey, deep in forest.

**Vascoeuil**
Art exhibition and cultural centre at feudal manor.

**Abbaye de Fontaine-Guérard**
Picturesque ruins by River Andelle.

*Woodman's cottage, Lyons-la-Forêt*

example, at Château-sur-Epte, Neaufles-St Martin and, far more substantially, at Gisors.

In its day, Gisors' fortress-château, overlooking the convergence of three valleys, was one of the strongest in the whole of France. Begun in 1097 by William Rufus, it was added to by subsequent kings on this turbulent border and became the mighty stronghold we can admire today, embodying three centuries of military building techniques.

Carefully preserved on its low hill in the town, curtain walls linking twelve towers enclose pleasant gardens and the great circular keep on its defensive mound in the centre. Inside the Prisoner's Tower, an oven, chimney and well can be found built into the thickness of wall. For those with imagination, history is brought vividly alive by prisoners' grafitti in the dungeon: names, dates, St George slaying the dragon and other poignant motifs from the fourteenth and fifteenth centuries are

carved into the soft stone.

Église St Gervais-et-St Protais, an impressive building dating back to the twelfth century, is undergoing restoration. A fine view of the church over the rooftops of narrow medieval houses can be obtained from the gardens inside the castle walls. Look out also for a seventeenth-century timbered wash-house on the river, and a bridge with the Virgin on the parapet.

The great Lyons beech forest, jealously preserved as a hunting ground by the Norman Dukes, covers the remaining corner of Eure and spills over into Seine-Maritime. The trees reach majestic proportions on the chalky soil, though tree cover is not continuous and the land is intermittently and intensively cultivated; wherever this occurs, however, always there is a dark edge of forest on the next ridge.

Individual trees have earned themselves reputations for size or longevity, such as the 300-year-old *Hêtre à Dieu* (God's Beech) between the Abbaye de Mortemer and Menesqueville, and *Hêtre de Bunodière*

— at 42m the tallest amongst many old specimens just off the N31 near Gournay-en-Bray. Timber is carefully harvested, tree-trunks lying like bundles of giant vegetables by the roadside. The entire 100sq km of forest is criss-crossed by *Routes Forestière,* tracks and footpaths.

Lyons-la-Forêt is an excellent centre for exploring the region on foot, on horseback or by car. A delicious little village full of colour-washed, half-timbered houses and very old inns, its reliance on wood as a building material

not only makes it look attractive, but also is supremely appropriate for a forest settlement. The eighteenth-century covered market, made from forest oaks, replaces a much earlier one and all but fills the village square, with its small complement of very good hotels and restaurants. The woodmen's fifteenth-century church has a timber belfry and many wooden statues.

Deep within the forest in the Fouillebroc valley, just to the south of Lyons-la-Forêt, stands one of the most powerfully evocative relics of medieval Christendom anywhere in France — Abbaye de Mortemer. Built in the twelfth century by Benedictine monks, it was later taken over and enlarged by a community of the Cistercian Order who retained it until the monks were dispersed and the abbey buildings desecrated after the French Revolution in 1790.

Many English and French monarchs stayed at the abbey: it is a site of historic significance and considerable beauty, well worth a special trip to see. It will be found to the left of the D715, 3km north of the village of Lisors, standing in a wooded depression by a lake. There is good car parking and entry is at the side of an adjacent farm. Though a fee is charged and visits are in guided groups only, there is a museum under the seventeenth-century reconstructed conventual building, and a look at it all is recommended.

For lovers of small country churches, Forêt de Lyons is dotted with interest. Suggested places forming the nucleus of a round tour include Lisors, Rosay-sur-Lieure, Menesqueville, Chapelle St Jean, la Feuillie and Beauficel-en-Lyons.

An international cultural centre which stages important art exhibitions is housed in the well restored feudal manor at Vascoeuil, right on the Seine-Maritime border at the confluence of the

*Abbaye de Fontaine-Guérard*

Crevon and Andelle rivers. For a time it was the residence of the French historian Michelet (1798-1874) — he wrote some of his epic *Histoire de France* here — and today its rich interior and architecture are popular with sightseeers. A more informative profile of Michelet is gained by visiting Maison Michelet, wherein are displayed letters, photographs and mementoes of this notable nineteenth-century scholar, his family and friends.

There are reconstructions of half-timbered, thatched Norman cottages in the attractive grounds.

Further south towards the Seine, the Andelle valley grows a little more industrialised, though this should be qualified by adding that picturesque countryside is always close at hand, as a drive up the Crevon valley will confirm.

South-east of the lively little town of Fleury-sur-Andelle, Ecouis stands on the last stretches of open Vexin between the Seine and Andelle. Its centre is dominated by the twin towers of its fourteenth-century collegiate church put up by Enguerrand de Marigny, a local lord and financial adviser to Philip the Fair. De Marigny was, tragically, hanged soon afterwards, but his encouragement of local artists and craftsmen resulted in the church receiving many works of art: it is now a fascinating museum of fourteenth to seventeenth century religious sculpture.

Close enough to the *Route des Abbayes* from Rouen to Le Havre to justify inclusion in any tour of these great religious monuments, Abbaye de Fontaine-Guérard is another hauntingly evocative ruin. Isolated amongst trees reflected in the River Andelle, the extensive twelfth-century abbey site is both enhanced and threatened by its proximity to the river, which has been known to flood.

Like Abbaye de Mortemer, an entry fee is charged and is again worth paying since, in addition to viewing sections of wall, graceful vaulting and the intact east end with its elegant windows, one can see at close quarters the Chapter House and climb a staircase to the monks' dormitory above the workroom. If the abbey entrance is closed, a view of the ruins is possible from a lane running uphill, also from the little bridge over the Andelle.

The itinerary has returned us to the Seine, now less than 10km away. By tracing its course to the sea, we arrive back at Eure's tiny and inauspicious stretch of coastline and move south into the department of Orne.

# 3 Orne

Orne is the only one of Normandy's departments to be land-locked, a region protected more than others from the prevailing Atlantic weather systems. Often there is more than a hint of France's great heartland in the warmer winds and sunshine found here: a taste of the Loire valley and beyond.

Of great cities there are none, of large towns but a few. Much of the countryside is well wooded and farmed — a more intimate *pot-pourri* of landscape features, lending itself to outdoor pursuits and country pastimes such as angling, riding, canoeing, walking, cycling and observing wildlife.

Held between the rivers Touques and Risle to the north lies the forested pays d'Ouche, while a little farther south is found the Perche. Steeper and dotted with small lakes, woods and villages, it is renowned for horse-breeding. The famous Percheron charger which bore armoured knights into battle originated here and can still be seen at the national stud near Argentan.

Historic castles, river gorges and several notable forests add their attractions to some fascinating settlements, from the sophisticated spa of Bagnoles-de-l'Orne to the ancient cathedral town of Sées.

For practical purposes, Orne will be divided into three sections: east, central and west, each dealt with separately. The dividing lines are, of course, imaginary and often blurred but provide a convenient framework around which the department can be described.

In the north-eastern corner of Orne stands Vimoutiers, a prolific producer of butter and cheese. Just 5km to the south in the village of Camembert, a farm woman by the name of Marie Harel perfected the soft cheese to which her village gave its name at the beginning of

*In the Forêt du Perche*

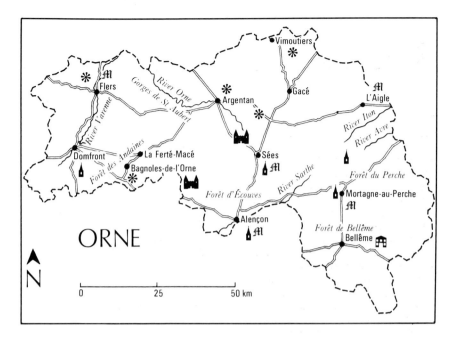

ORNE

the nineteenth century. Vimoutiers, indeed, is something of a gastronomic centre for the Orne, being concerned also with the production of Calvados, a distilled apple brandy traditionally taken between courses in a meal and more usually associated with the Auge region just to the north. A society dedicated to the promotion of Calvados — Les Chevaliers du Trou-Normand — is based in the town, and a distillery can be visited.

Vimoutiers' remaining old buildings represent many facets of Norman architecture: there is a half-timbered mill in the town centre, the remains of a sixteenth-century convent, and a fine church by the River Vie. Elsewhere, considerable war damage in 1944 resulted in some fairly extensive rebuilding.

Pays d'Ouche is a close neighbour of pays d'Auge and shares some of its picturesqueness: orchards, cattle, timber-and-wattle farm houses reminiscent of Tudor England. However, the wooded plateau farther south, drained by the Risle, was once a thriving quarry area for the red iron agglomerate then used in buidling.

Near the border with Eure, between pays d'Ouche and the Perche, the town of l'Aigle maintains in its modern steel-drawing mills a tradition of metal-working once the domain of hundreds of small forges in villages like Rai and Rugles. It is one of the upper Risle's largest towns and is a market centre for

PLACES OF INTEREST IN NORTH-EASTERN ORNE

**Vimoutiers**
Calvados (apple-brandy) Distillery in gastronomic centre. Also old Norman mill, ruined sixteenth-century Convent.

**Camembert village**
Home of the famous soft cheese.

**L'Aigle**
World War II Museum: wax figures and recorded voices.

*The fortified manor-house of Courboyer*

the Perche region, on which it borders.
(A large market is held each Tuesday.)
Église St Martin is a mixture of old and
new, parts dating back to the eleventh
century. The modern statues in niches
between the windows of the south nave
are by the father of French film star
Jean-Paul Belmondo, and there is also a
series of contemporary stained glass
windows.

Next to the Hôtel-de-Ville may be
found a small museum (*Juin 44: Bataille
de Normandie*), devoted to the
development of the Battle of Normandy.
There are wax figures and the recorded
voices of leading politicians, including
Churchill, Stalin, de Gaulle and
Roosevelt.

South of l'Aigle is the Perche, an
undulating countryside of complicated
geological structure, situated between
the Paris Basin and the Armorican
Massif. Soils are mainly non-porous and
a moist climate encourages a dense cover

of oak and beech on the primary
limestone, with fertile arable land and
pastures on the secondary marls and
clays. It is an area of woods and rivers,
of small farmsteads and horses.

Mellow, warm-stone manor houses,
some resembling small castles, stand
back a short distance from roads. Built
in the fifteenth and sixteenth centuries
— substantial, fortified places — they
are now mostly farmhouses, though
their turrets and great round towers are
still impressive features.

Just off the D930 half way between
l'Aigle and Mortagne-au-Perche, the
Abbaye de la Grande Trappe is
approached along a lovely tree-lined
avenue and stands alone in the forest
near many delightful small lakes and the
private Étang de Chaumont. The abbey,
founded in 1140, initiated the re-
establishment of the Trappist Order, the
origin of the existing strict Cistercian
Order, in the eighteenth century.

Visitors are shown round and an audio-visual presentation paints a picture of monastic life. To enter the building, contact Frère Portier (doorkeeper).

Near the start of the Avre valley, 12km north-east of Mortagne-au-Perche, the little unassuming town of Tourouvre provides a good centre for walking and exploring in the Forêt du Perche. Its *Syndicat d'Initiative* occupies the church porch, whilst inside can still be found fifteenth-century choir stalls and an 'Adoration of the Magi' painting from the same period above the altar.

A road just west of the church leads steeply uphill into forest, once extensively hunted and criss-crossed by rides. Forest roads now radiate from Carrefour de l'Étoile ('Crossroads of the Star') like spokes in a wheel, providing a number of pleasant excursions and starting points for rambles. A chain of *étangs* (lakes), one of several in the region, leads north-east, and one lake near Bresolettes reflects the white Château des Étangs in its dark, tree-shaded waters.

There are splendid views over the Perche from the hilltop market town of Mortagne-au-Perche, home of the Percheron and famous for horse-breeding. The town, with its distinctive brown-tiled roofs, has expanded greatly since the fifteenth century and most of its original fortifications have disappeared: Porte St Denis, in the centre, is almost all that remains, the existing arch having once supported a two-storey building.

The adjacent Flamboyant Gothic and early Renaissance Église Notre-Dame is noted for its outstanding woodcarving on the choir stalls, pulpit and altarpiece panels, all of which came from the Valdieu Carthusian Monastery in the Forêt de Reno Valdieu to the east of Mortagne. Only a few traces now remain. The church's sixteenth-century cloister is also well worth seeing (apply at the porter's lodge in Chemin du Cloître).

Mortagne is a good touring centre, with a pleasant ambience and lively shopping streets. From its attractive Jardin Public by the bus station, there are wide-ranging views and elsewhere amenities exist for tennis, swimming and riding. There is a small museum of the Perche region and, if you happen to be here in March, look out for the Black Pudding Fair!

By taking minor roads to the east and swinging south-west to Bellême, a comprehensive picture of the Perche region emerges. La Goyère castle is passed on the right, in hilly countryside, before entering the Forêt de Reno-Valdieu, with its stands of ancient oaks and beeches. The small town of Longny-au-Perche, set close to the lake-dotted forest of the same name, has two churches, one of which — Notre-Dame-de-Pitié — is distinguished by beautiful wooden doors carved by a local craftsman in the nineteenth century.

Feillet manor, just beyond le Mage

---

**PLACES OF INTEREST IN THE PERCHE REGION**

**Abbaye de la Grande Trappe**
In lake-dotted forest. Audio-visual presentation of monastic life.

Walking and touring in lovely Forêt du Perche, based perhaps on Tourouvre.

**Mortagne-au-Perche**
Old market town: outstanding woodcarving in Notre-Dame church; also museum, sports amenities, attractive public gardens and shopping streets.

Numerous fortified manor-houses — Courboyer, south of Bellême, most impressive.

Medieval walled town of Bellême and its large oak forest — signed walks and drives.

village, leads on to Moutiers-au-Perche in its pretty valley setting; more picturesque countryside, green and undulating, brings us round past Remalard to two junctions left for Nocé. From both these D roads there are good views of one of the Perche's most impressive fortified manor-houses — Courboyer. Built of pale stone in the fifteenth century, it stands at the side of a shallow, lush valley, its four graceful watchtowers and a massive round tower surmounted by conical slate roofs.

To the south, Ste Gauburge's deconsecrated Gothic church is now a Museum of Popular Art and Tradition; behind the building are the remains of a former priory, converted to a farmhouse and not open to the public but worth a look for its fine pentagonal tower.

Angenardière manor — a large, evocatively feudal edifice — and Feugerets castle complete the round tour of the district, ending in Bellême, capital of the Perche.

Built on ancient crossroads 225m above extensive forest, the little fortified town has retained its medieval character, with several narrow alleyways and old, colourfully-shuttered houses reflected in the moat (especially nos 24 and 26, Rue Ville-Close). Access to Ville Close is through the thirteenth-century city gate, *Le Porche,* flanked by two towers and swans nesting on a nearby pond!

The Forêt de Bellême is predominantly oak — 5930 acres of it — and there are good retrospective views of the town from the north on D938. Worthwhile walks abound here, including a short one round Étang de la Herse. An unsurfaced forestry road winds east to the Étoile de la Reine Blanche and the delightful Creux valley.

For visitors on wheels, a *Route Touristique* has been signposted through the forest to la Perrière, a curiously ramshackle village on a hill at the forest edge. There is a spectacular panorama over the Perche from its church courtyard, extending in good visibility to the Forêt de Perseigne and even as far west as the Forêt d'Écouves.

The imaginary border with the central section of the Orne department, running north to Argentan, has been reached. The departmental border itself draws a semicircular line above the Forêt de Perseigne — a loss for Normandy and certainly worth visiting if staying in the Alençon area.

At the centre of fertile countryside in the upper valley of the Sarthe, Alençon is a large agricultural market town and capital of Orne. Its history was linked for centuries with the powerful and tragic Dukes of Alençon, though their fourteenth-century fortress (now a prison) at the edge of a town centre park is the only significant relic. There is, however, much medieval town architecture for the visitor to seek out, notably Maison d'Oze, a well restored fifteenth-century house containing Gallo-Roman antiquities, exhibits from Cambodia, paintings and a coin collection. Perhaps Alençon's finest building is the church of Notre-Dame, a beautiful fourteenth-century structure with an elegant, three-sided porch; tower and choirs were rebuilt in the eighteenth century.

The town has been renowned for lace-making since the seventeenth century when Louis XIV's Chancellor, Colbert, decided to restrict imports of popular Venetian lace. A state-run school of lace-making — *École Dentellière,* on Rue

---

### Places of Interest in Sées

**Cathédrale St Latrium**
High twin spires, magnificent architecture, thirteenth-century stained-glass. Folk Museum in Chapter House. *Son-et-lumière* in summer.

Several interesting churches.

**Museum of French Religious Art**
In old abbey buildings.

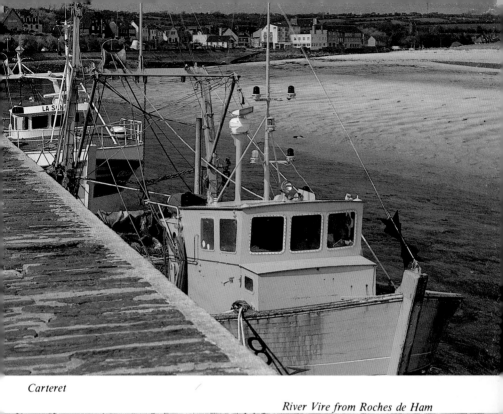

*Carteret*

*River Vire from Roches de Ham*

*Château d'Angotière*

*Granville harbour*

de Pont-Neuf by the River Sarthe — provides visitors with an opportunity to see lace being made and to inspect and purchase items if desired. On display there is a veil worn by Marie Antoinette. Further material on Alençon's lace-making industry, including some rare examples, may be viewed in a museum at the imposing Hôtel-de-Ville, which also houses a good art gallery, the Musée de Peinture; Place Foch, in which it stands, is a large car parking area. The town has good shops and restaurants, facilities for tennis, swimming and riding, an ice-rink, and markets held each Thursday, Friday and Sunday.

Forêt d'Écouves, 37,000 acres of magnificent oak, beech and conifers (mainly Norman pine and spruce) lies within the huge Parc Naturel Régional Normandie-Maine. This designated area of outstanding natural beauty covers 585,000 acres in southern Normandy and the Sarthe, stretching north-west to south-east from Mortain to Sille-le-Guillaume near Le Mans.

Far from containing principally uninhabited and wild open country, these French Regional Nature Parks are simply intended to protect an area's special heritage from harmful exploitation. Thus, while new industrial development is not permitted, people do live and work within the parks which often contain sizeable towns, in this instance La Ferté-Macé, Domfront and Carrouges.

Parc Régional Normandie-Maine is a haven for cyclists and walkers, with numerous minor roads and footpaths crossing it. Several long-distance walking trails also cross the park and there is wide scope for day-walking. Useful information, maps and topo-guides can usually be obtained from local *Syndicats d'Initiative*.

The Forêt d'Écouves clothes a granite crest rising to over 400m, the Signal d'Écouves beacon at 417m sharing its distinction as the highest point in western France with Mont des Avaloirs, just outside Normandy to the south-west. A network of tracks branch through the forest and it is sometimes possible to glimpse the deer and roebuck which roam freely here, though they are hunted during the winter.

Yellow waymarks lead from the D26 to the Rochers du Vignage, a low rocky ridge giving splendid prospects across the forest; the path returns to the road higher up. 3km west lies la Croix-Madame crossroads with its ancient milestone and stand of Norman pines. There is yet more scope for pleasant forest walks here, including the Sapaie Pichon path, marked with yellow flashes.

Another milestone, octagonal and etched with old road names, marks la Croix-de-Médavy junction, 5km to the north-east; more conspicuous, however, is a commemorative tank installed in memory of the French 2nd Armoured Division under General Leclerc which cleared the forest of Germans in August 1944.

Anyone by-passing Sées on the N158 will catch a tantalisingly beautiful view of its twin-spired cathedral rising above serried ranks of roofs. It is a place that should not be missed; a charming little town, calm and quiet for much of the year, so rich with old buildings that time almost seems to have stood still.

Cathédrale St Latrium is all-dominating. Its two spires, reaching to over 60m in height, are conspicuous for miles around, incongruously appearing over fields and low ridges. The original cathedral building was destroyed by Norman marauders and what we see today is a twelfth to fourteenth-century Norman Gothic replacement, one of the best of its kind. There is a magnificent, if crumbling, main doorway with great soaring Norman arches, and an older unused doorway to the right. In fact, to prevent further dangerous subsidence, the main façade porch was heavily buttressed in the sixteenth century, though whether this feature is as seriously disfiguring as some claim is open to debate.

*The cathedral town of Sées*

---

Within are some very fine thirteenth-century stained glass windows and a fourteenth-century statue of Notre-Dame-de-Sées. There is a Folk Museum in the Chapter House and *son-et-lumière* shows at summer weekends.

During the fifth century, Sées was a bishopric and contains some interesting churches, notably Notre-Dame-de-la-Place in Rue St Martin, and the Ancien Abbaye St Martin which houses a Musée d'Art Religieux devoted to French religious art through the centuries. The old Bishop's Palace (*Ancien Évêché*) adjacent to the cathedral is not open to the public but is worth looking at, as is the Hôtel-de-Ville.

In common with many rural French towns, Sées appears comfortably faded, its streets a touch down-at-heel, but perhaps any brasher ambience would betray its historical character. For information on the town and locality, visit the helpful *Syndicat d'Initiative.*

7km north-west of Sées stands the best known of all Orne Châteaux. Until fairly recently, Château d'O was used as a children's home and is only now being restored; its main living quarters were completely rebuilt in the eighteenth century. For all that, it is an immensely elegant and romantic building, originally late fifteenth century and showing well the transition from Gothic to early Renaissance architecture. Virtually free of military features, its chequerboard ornamentation, highly decorated turrets and steep slate roofs are reflected in a broad moat spanned by the narrow access bridge, while all around stretches peaceful parkland. A delightful place to visit, perhaps picnicking by the lake with its complement of swans, or strolling in the grounds. The adjacent Ferme d'O may also be visited.

French reverence and enthusiasm for the breeding of fine horses finds expression in the national stud at Haras-du-Pin, sometimes dubbed the 'Versailles of the Horse'. This prestigious establishment, occupying a château designed by Mansart, was started in the late seventeenth century by

*Château d'O*

*View over Suisse Normande from Roche d'Oëtre*

Colbert. Today, its stables house over eighty stallions — from English thoroughbreds to Norman cobs, from French trotters to the noble Percheron.

Tours are conducted every half-hour in season, though it is worth noting that the full complement of stallions is at the stud only between mid-July and mid-February. Additionally, horses may be watched departing for and arriving back from their daily exercise. Horse-racing takes place at the nearby Pin-au-Haras Hippodrome during July, September and October (details from the *Syndicat d'Initiative* or local press), with carriage processions on the first Sunday in September and the second Sunday in October.

Argentan, built mainly on the west bank of the River Orne, was close to the scene of the last battle for Normandy in August 1944, sustaining heavy damage. It was almost entirely reconstructed and there is much nondescript post-war development — an apparent disincentive to the visitor seeking tangible evidence of its history.

Like Alençon, however, Argentan was once a lace-making centre of some note and here, too, the craft is kept alive. At the Benedictine Abbey, (2 Rue de l'Abbaye), nuns run a lace workshop and there is a museum of stitch-lace showing the unique 'Point d'Argentan' stitch, to which the nuns have exclusive rights: it was created here and is a feature of the work produced.

The town's two churches did not escape wartime shelling, but restoration has made good some of the damage. The

fifteenth to seventeenth century Église St
Germain has a fine Flamboyant porch
opening on to Rue St Germain, amongst
other interesting features. Église St
Martin's spire was truncated by shelling
but its octagonal tower and excellent
sixteenth-century stained glass are still
intact.

On the south side of Place St Germain
stand the remnants of a fourteenth-
century castle which belonged to the
Dukes of Alençon; there are good views
of the town from a *table d'orientation* on
its tower.

Five châteaux can be reached within
about a dozen kilometres of Argentan,
making a stay here almost obligatory for
lovers of historic buildings! Eighteenth-
century Le Bourg-St Léonard lies 12km
east amid pleasant parkland, and
contains fine tapestries and
contemporary furniture. The twelfth-
century medieval château-fortress of
Chambois, 12km north-east, overlooks
ground where the Allies joined together
on 19 August 1944, trapping the
German 7th Army in what became
known as the 'Falaise Pocket' (an
obelisk marks the spot). Château de
Rânes, 15km south-west, dominates the

village and dates from the fifteenth
century, with gardens by Le Nôtre. The
present Château de Médavy was built
around 1700 by the Grancey family who
still occupy it, but a castle has stood on
the same site since the eleventh century
(a few traces still exist, notably the gate
towers). Finally, at the edge of a sizeable
lake, Château de Sassy will be found
9km south of Argentan; its gardens are
magnificent and the library, chapel and
tapestries are all worth seeing.

Moving east past the little old town of
Putanges-Pont-Ecrepin, we enter the last
section of Orne department, towards its
western border with Manche. Most of
the 'Suisse Normande' lies in the
department of Calvados; however, its
most southerly features spill over into
Orne.

Putanges-Pont-Ecrepin makes a good
starting point for exploration on foot of
the St Aubert gorges, created where the
River Orne cuts through ancient rocks of
the Armorican Massif. By narrow road
west from Rabodanges, and a quarter of
an hour walk, Moulin de la Jalousie is
reached, isolated mill ruins facing the
site of the ancient Devil's Bridge. Nearer
the village is a seventeenth-century castle
in parkland overlooking the Orne valley,
while to the south may by found a multi-
arch dam with a *bélvèdere* on the right

bank — the Barrage de Rabodange.

Dominating the wild, winding Rouvre Gorges is southern Normandy's most mountainous feature — Roche d'Oëtre. This sensational lip of vegetated grey-brown cliff 120m above the Orne's densely wooded valley is only a stone's throw from the D301 road. A bar/créperie and carpark cater for visitors and, although the rock-edge is indicated by signposts, it is quite an airy perch. Care is needed, especially with children or in wet and windy weather.

From the tourist crossroad town of Pont d'Ouilly, the departmental border follows the River Noireau west, running beneath high escarpments to the village of Pont-Erambourg, where the waters of the Vère and Noireau meet. Leading south towards Flers, the River Vère's course grows progressively narrower and swifter-flowing.

Flers was a textile town until the industry went into decline; factories to the north, on the site of old ironworks, were later cotton mills and now house modern light industries. Though not outwardly concerned with tourism, Flers nevertheless makes a good base from which to visit the Suisse Normande and the *bocage* to the west.

The château's sixteenth-century towers and its shady parkland surroundings are reflected in a moat and pond: it is a quite unusual building, with a Classical main façade. The town's museum displays a collection of seventeenth to nineteenth century paintings and exhibits to do with cotton-weaving, farming and local life, as well as specimens of palaeontology and minerals.

place here. The occupying German forces were able to resist the Allied advance in such ideal defensive terrain and for a while it was halted. The nightmare prospect of combat in such difficult countryside, where closely-knit fields and hedgerows acted as an obstacle course to progress and ready-made cover for the enemy, can only be imagined by those who did not experience it.

Domfront stands on a long, rocky ridge above the River Varenne, almost at the heart of the *bocage*. A small, rather straggling medieval border town, it was once a vigorously contested strategic strongpoint belonging to the notorious Bellême family. Today it is a well-visited place surrounded by a landscape of apple orchards.

When its half-timbered streets echo to the unwelcome sound of 'Muzak', the town can seem a trifle tawdry, though this impression is quickly dispelled by a

---

**EXCURSIONS AROUND FLERS AND DOMFRONT**

**St Aubert gorges**
On River Orne to the north-east. Also Roche d'Oëtre, Normandy's most mountainous feature.

**Mont-Cerisi**
To the north-west for extensive views and river walk.

**Historic Domfront**
On ridge above *bocage*. Old buildings, beautiful cruciform Romanesque Notre-Dame-de-l'Eau by river.

Surrounding countryside contains some forty fifteenth and sixteenth-century manor-houses and picturesque Norman farmsteads.

---

A short excursion can be made north-west to Mont Cerisi, reached along a rhododendron-lined toll road off the D18 from the village of Cerisi-Belle-Étoile. From the summit (260m), there are extensive views over the *bocage* and the distant hills of the Suisse Normande. A little further along the D18, a left turn over the River Noireau takes a narrow track between Mont Cerisi and the St Pierre rocks to Les Vaux, a scenic hollow; the route can be extended on foot.

The *bocage* overlaps from Calvados and eastern Manche into Orne and is a distinct landscape, peculiar to this part of Normandy. Woodland, small meadows and orchards are enclosed within a matrix of high banks and impenetrable hedges. Some of the fiercest fighting of World War II took

visit to its delightful historic sites. Only two walls of the castle keep remain standing — it was dismantled in the seventeenth century and the ground was laid out as gardens. However, many of the thirteen original rampart towers are intact and provide fascinating views over narrow streets, old roofs and gateways and the *bocage* below.

St Julien is a twentieth-century church and its kitschy modern interior bears no comparison in either quality or design to those of previous eras. By contrast, Notre-Dame-sur-l'Eau, on the riverbank beneath Domfront, is worthy of a special visit. Dating from 1050, this beautiful little cruciform Romanesque church where Thomas-à-Becket is reputed to have said Mass, was foreshortened in the nineteenth century to make way for the modern road. Its simple proportions were not drastically affected and it remains a gem of its kind, containing several interesting tombs.

Within a radius of about 10km are some forty picturesque fifteenth and sixteenth century manor-houses in attractive farmland settings. That they are still within the Parc Régional Normandie-Maine comes as no surprise, considering the qualities of landscape to be found in this region.

Orne as a department is not well endowed with resorts — places nourished by tourism and concerned with the tastes and needs of visitors. Towns and countryside do possess much of interest, to be sure, but one has the feeling that it is all seen as a sideline, a distraction, almost, from the day-to-day business of earning a living. Tourism, on the whole, is simply not courted and where activities are openly encouraged, they tend to be of the outdoor kind, for an outdoor region. But Bagnoles-de-l'Orne is an exception.

This popular spa, largest in western France, enjoyed royal patronage as far back as the sixth century, and by the Edwardian era was immensely fashionable. Bagnoles' inevitable decline since those heady days has been slowed,

if not halted, by its growing reputation as a rejuvenating spa; sulphuric and radioactive baths purportedly curing circulatory and glandular disorders. This new lease on life, however, is not proving to be the town's hoped-for salvation and there is an increasing need to attract healthy tourists in addition to those requiring treatment.

Bagnoles is an extremely pleasant, cosmopolitan place, replete with expensive restaurants, *salons de thé* and high-class shops. Dante Avenue, on the left bank of the Vée, is often crowded with bathers and leads to the spa building itself, patronised by many well-heeled Europeans: the air is heavy with expensive perfume and the swish of costly clothes!

Water from the Great Spring gushes forth at a constant 27°C (80°F) and at a flow-rate of 11,000 gallons an hour. It is the only hot spring in this part of France.

A white casino and luxury hotels fringe a lovely town-centre lake, whose

---

### PLACES OF INTEREST IN AND AROUND BAGNOLES-DE-L'ORNE

**Bagnoles-de-l'Orne**
Mineral spa from only hot spring in this part of France; town-centre lake, gardens and casino; many sporting amenities, good shops and restaurants.

**Surrounding Andaines forest**
Waymarked walking and riding trails. Wildlife, gorges, lakes, rocky outcrops, chapels.

**La Ferté-Macé**
Cobbled streets, good market, less expensive!

To the east — wonderful sixteenth-century red-brick Château de Carrouges in grounds; richly furnished interior with portrait gallery.

*The gatehouse, Château de Carrouges*

shores are laid out with gardens and willows. Boating, walking and riding are only a few of the outdoor activities possible in and around Bagnoles: its situation at the mouth of a gorge on the southern edge of the glorious Forêt des Andaines makes it an ideal choice for an active holiday. Sporting provision is generous, including tennis, swimming, shooting, fishing and golf. Perhaps because of its distinctive character, the town seems busy throughout the year, with the influx of visitors reaching a peak in July and August.

The mixed Forêt Domaniaux des Andaines is of major amenity value to the area and its leisure use is encouraged. 32km of metalled road cross it, as does double that amount of rough forestry tracks, not all suitable for vehicles. 13 walking trails have been waymarked, totalling 43km in length — most are about 2 to 3 hours long. Horse-riding itineraries are also being established.

There are numerous sights within the forest: the gorges of Villiers and the Vée; the lakes of la Cour, la Forge, l'Ermitage and Prise Pontin; rocky outcrops at Mont-en-Gérome, Roche aux Loups and Rocher Broutin; and the chapels of St Ortaire, St Antoine, Friches and Ste Geneviève. Like many natural habitats, the Andaines forest is vulnerable to abuse by carelessness; fire is a real threat and wildlife can easily be disturbed by noisy or thoughtless behaviour.

Details of forest trails and events in or near Bagnoles can be obtained from the excellent *Maison du Tourisme.*

7km west, just south of the forest, an extraordinary double tower, one part tall and unequivocally phallic, rises above the landscape. *Phare de Bonvouloir,* a former chapel, dovecote and well was erected in the fifteenth century by the Lord of Bonvouloir to celebrate the restoration of his potency by the Bagnoles spa waters!

As different as chalk and cheese, la Ferté-Macé — a mere 6km north of Bagnoles — is a charming old town of grey-brown stone, famed for a local gastronomic delicacy, *tripe-en-brochette,* strips of tripe cooked on skewers. Cobbled streets are partly pedestrianised and there is a very good Thursday market. An ornate façade, unusually colourful, marks the modern church's main structure, but the tower is, unexpectedly, eleventh century. Works by local artist Léandre de la Touche can be viewed in the Musée Municipal. La Ferté-Macé would be a good alternative centre to Bagnoles — a little less expensive and a little quieter, especially in high season.

The final port of call, and an essential one for any visitor to Orne, is Carrouges, 17km east of la Ferté-Macé. The small, attractive village, set on a low hill, is the centre for Parc Régional Normandie-Maine which it administers from Maison du Parc in the old castle. Information on all outdoor activities within the park is available through this office.

Fortified in the twelfth century by the Counts of Carrouges, who retained control until 1450, the village passed into the hands of the Tillières family and remained theirs until as recently as 1936. Its principal attraction is a quite outstanding château one kilometre to the south: a sight not to be missed! Set amidst tree-dotted lawns near the River Udon and surrounded by a moat, this massive, rose-red brick-and-stone edifice is approached through an elegant gateway, itself a remarkable sight with high conical slate roofs and decorative brickwork.

Château de Carrouges impresses in a way few other buildings do. Constructed by the powerful Tillières family in the sixteenth century, to replace an ancestral twelfth-century fortress, it appears almost untouched by the intervening years. Four circular towers capped with pepperpot roofs, rows of elaborate Renaissance windows, lovely formal gardens and avenues of chestnut trees conspire to provide an impression of perfection, as if all the elements of proportion, colour, texture and pattern are miraculously without blemish.

Despite being now owned by the state, no attempt has been made to exploit the château, the only concession being hour-long guided tours of the interior. Among many diverse features are opulent furnishings, seventeenth-century paintings and a portrait gallery. For most of the year, Château de Carrouges is free of crowds — a tranquil and inspiring spot.

# 4 Calvados

Calvados must rank as Normandy's most diverse department, a rich interweaving of history and tradition with natural beauty and modern facilites. Its name is reputed to be a corruption of 'Salvador', a Spanish ship sunk on rocks off Arromanches while running for home after defeat in 1588.

Following the D-Day landings of World War II, the Calvados coast became legendary and remains today a place of pilgrimage. It is visited by a never-ending stream of people from all nations, intent on seeing for themselves the beaches on which the landings took place, the war museums and the great military cemeteries — vivid reminders of a tragic conflict which laid its hand heavily on this part of France.

Elsewhere along the open, sandy coastline are myriad attractions, from quaint Honfleur to fashionable Deauville, from fishing harbours like Port-en-Bessin to family resorts like Riva-Bella or Courseulles-sur-Mer.

Just inland lies the picturesque pays d'Auge, an undulating region of orchards and meadows, of chalk river valleys, woodland and delectable little villages. Pays d'Auge is renowned for its cheeses, cider and apple brandy and contains perhaps the most quintessentially Norman scenery to be found anywhere in the province. In addition, Calvados as a whole is scattered with magnificent châteaux and manor houses, many of which are connected by 'round-tour' itineraries.

Basse Normandie is centred on the historic city of Caen, ancient capital of

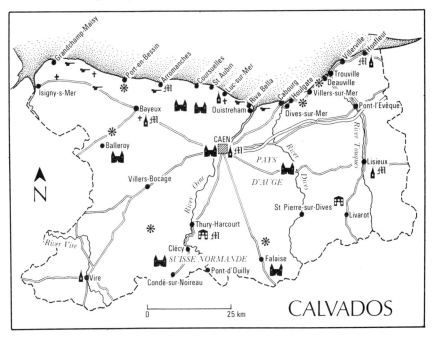

CALVADOS

*Église Ste Catherine across Honfleur's Vieux Bassin*

the Norman Dukes. A short distance
away to the east may be found the
famous Bayeux tapestry, housed in a
special museum and drawing many
thousands of visitors each year.

The countryside flattens and opens
out into a rolling plain towards the
southern border with Orne and the
marvellous old town of Falaise. To the
west, however, the landscape grows
more intimate again in a complex of
fields and woods enclosed by high
hedges or banks; it is known as the
*bocage* and was the scene of bitter
fighting in World War II as the Allied

advance was held at bay for a time by
German forces in this perfect defensive
terrain.

Further west still, bordering the River
Vire at the foot of the Cotentin
Peninsula, lies the Bessin, rich pasture
yielding the dairy products which have
earned Calvados its reputation as one of
France's finest gastronomic regions.

Finally, shared with the neighbouring
department of Orne, the so-called Suisse
Normande provides a haven for walkers,
canoeists, cyclists and anglers in its
jumble of steep-sided hills between
meandering river valleys. Reference to

Switzerland is a trifle misleading, since no summit exceeds 365m, but from the hilltops and encircling roads there are superb views of this soft and rolling country.

The exploration of Calvados begins in the east at its border with Eure, and moves west across the department. Major rivers (the Touques, Dives, Orne and Vire) lead inland, as most are aligned north-south; the coast may thus be taken in portions between river mouths.

Honfleur sits on the Seine estuary opposite pastel-hued oil storage tanks near Le Havre — pretty enough at a distance! — and from its rather unlovely beach, reached by tunnel beneath the coast road, one can watch large ships at close quarters leaving and entering this busy river mouth.

In considerable contrast to its northern aspect, Honfleur itself is a delightful place to visit and has for long been a favourite with the British. There are quaint old cobbled streets, public gardens, a museum of local history and the quite extraordinary timber church of Ste Catherine.

Such a building, with its separate belfry clad in chestnut weatherboarding, is rare in western Europe, and may have been intended as a temporary solution to rebuilding following the departure of the English after the Hundred Years' War. It is said that local shipwrights, eager to put the church up, simply could not wait for stone to be found, opting instead for

*Quayside artist, Honfleur*

*Cricqueboeuf's twelfth-century church*

the timber to which they were so
accustomed and which was freely
available. The interior is interesting too,
containing many carvings and statues.

Samuel Champlain, an expert
seventeenth-century navigator, set sail
from Honfleur with orders from
François I to colonise the territory
known as Canada, which had been
claimed nearly 100 years before by
Jacques Cartier of Dieppe. Champlain
duly founded Quebec in 1608, and
Canada's development began virtually

as a Norman colony. A plaque
commemorating Champlain's departure
can be found on the harbour.

During the emergence of
Impressionism in the latter part of the
nineteenth century, this corner of
Normandy embracing the pays de Caux
coast, the Seine estuary, the Côte de
Grâce and Rouen became a focal point,
a source of visual inspiration. Artists
congregated at Honfleur, in the St
Siméon bar at Mère Toutain's.

Eugène Boudin was a native of the

town and the museum gallery named
after him contains many interesting
works of the period. Other artists
represented include Monet, Corot, Huet,
Courbet, as well as 'foreigners' such as
Bonington and Jongkind. Writers and
musicians were here too, among them
Baudelaire and Erik Satie, who was born
at 90, Rue Haute.

Honfleur's artistic heritage owes
everything to the creative energy and
formal innovations of the late 1800s, and
today's art galleries, it must be said, lean
heavily on that reputation. On the
whole, the quayside artists with their
easels and straw hats are but a faded
echo of that once vigorous movement:
one suspects the show is largely for the
tourists. And of tourists there are many,
attracted by quayside cafés and
shopping streets around the Vieux
Bassin — the Old Dock. A few colourful
fishing boats still moor up here but the
once considerable fleet has been
replaced by pleasure craft, a dazzle of
hulls, rigging and flags reflected in the
dock's water. Beyond their masts rise
terraces of narrow, slate-faced houses up
to seven storeys high — tall, princely
buildings invoking a flavour of the Low
Countries and adding to a pervasive
mellowness of texture and colour.

Restaurants serve delicious seafood,
which is also on sale at quayside stalls
along with fruit and vegetables,
although prices can be inflated during
the summer season: an almost inevitable
consequence of Honfleur's popularity.

A little to the west rises the Côte de
Grâce, a wooded hilltop providing
marvellous panoramas from its Calvary
and the Mont Joli viewpoint, extending
across to Le Havre and the Pont de
Tancarville. Seventeenth-century Notre-
Dame-de-Grâce, replacing an earlier
sanctuary reputed to have been founded
in the eleventh century by Robert le
Diable, was visited by explorers and
navigators from the region who came to
pray before setting out on expeditions of
discovery and colonisation to North
America. A Seamen's Festival on Whit
Sunday and Monday each year sustains
this maritime tradition with a Blessing of
the Sea, a procession of seamen and
children with model ships, and Mass in
front of the chapel.

Narrow, uneven and crowded in high
season, the little D513 coast road is
nevertheless a scenic drive, dubbed the
'Normandy Corniche'. Through gaps in
orchards and hedges bordering its
twisting course are wide views of the
Seine estuary, while inland it passes
picturesque cottages whose thatched
roofs are bright with gladioli.

At the village of Criqueboeuf, on a
bend in the road about a kilometre east
of Villerville, stands a lovely little ivy-
clad twelfth-century church with a
simple stone interior. It is best viewed
looking back from a pull-in just beyond
the bend.

Villerville manages to combine
liveliness during the season with
unpretentiousness — a characteristic of
many Norman seaside resorts. Dropping
steeply to the sea, there are more views

to Le Havre and Cap de la Hève, while
at low tide the Ratier Bank becomes
uncovered, revealing mussel beds and
rock pools.

Trouville, one of France's oldest
'summer stations' dating back to 1852
and the Second Empire, rubs elbows
with its glamorous sister resort of
Deauville at the mouth of the River
Touques. When banks close in one, they
open in the other, but although the two
towns complement one another in a
number of ways, there are many

significant differences.

Trouville's origins as a pretty fishing
village pre-date Deauville's by a decade
or more. Its stature grew around the
turn of the century as artists and writers
came here, enhancing the town's
reputation and attracting the wealthy.
Progressively, however, Deauville stole
the limelight and Trouville found itself
something of the poor relation,
concerned more with commerce and
fishing, unable to compete with the
growing popularity of Deauville's

A wooden promenade ('les Planches') at the back of a vast sandy beach is lined by Gothic villas, beach clubs, a swimming pool and mini-golf, with ample space for everyone. Red and green lighthouses mark the ends of two timber jetties each side of the River Touques' mouth: currents here are dangerous, as are the jetties themselves in rough sea conditions, though at other times they provide pleasant strolls and wide coastal views.

Seafront architecture is dominated by the huge Casino and Thalassotherapy centre (sea-water cures) — an immaculate white complex of grandiose proportions. The riverside Hôtel-de-Ville is another dazzling white confection. Shops, bars and restaurants are lively and the quaysides worth looking at for an imposing neo-Norman *Poissonerie* (fish-market) and fishing boats moored up in the river. A footbridge connects with Deauville at low tide, a ferry at other times.

Public buildings include the Musée Montebello, with work by Eugène Boudin, Jongkind, Isabey and others, and the churches of Notre-Dame-des-Victoires, Bon-Secours and St Michel. Markets are held on Wednesday and Sunday off season, daily from Whitsun to September.

For those who have witnessed Deauville in the full swing of summer, a midweek encounter out of season may well surprise and disappoint. Each side of an annual two months of concentrated activity sees only a thin scattering of visitors, and without these Deauville has no razmataz and little chic. Beach cabins, restaurants and bars are closed, mini-golf abandoned, ponies riderless, while acres of tennis courts stand unused. Many villas are bolted and shuttered, the marina's forest of white yachts deserted: a hundred *Marie Celestes*!

In wintertime, Deauville seems even

sporting amenities and social high-life.

Today, there is irony in Trouville's comparative decline as a destination for the rich and famous. Its fishing and commercial interests keep the town alive when the season is over and when smarter resorts, deprived of the lifeblood of tourism, have submitted to a kind of living death.

Lest the wrong impression of Trouville be given, it is a fine family resort in its own right, picturesquely placed on high ground above the river.

less appealing. It lies in windswept suspended animation, except for fine weekends when a small tide of *Tout Paris* — the Paris rich — is moved to take the air! The town's shops and restaurants retain their exclusive tag for the benefit of city visitors, high summer prices reflecting their need to make hay while the sun shines.

Perhaps more than any other signals that the season has begun, the most telling is the unfurling of flags along les Planches and the visual explosion of brightly-hued beach tents. There is something enduringly cheery about all that colour: a foil, maybe, for otherwise featureless sands and an ever-distant sea.

The famous seafront promenade of timber decking — les Planches — is of limited interest without the well-to-do, the celebrated, the aspiring and the ordinarily curious who conspire so well to entertain each other by parading up and down. It is a tradition of mutual inspection more typically Levantine than Norman, but then Deauville has long associations with a clientele equally at home in Cannes or Nice. Among

The beach, Deauville

82

those who have associated themselves with this eminently modish place are Elié de Rothschild, the Aga Khan, the Dolly sisters, Pulitzer, Rockefeller, André Citroën, King Farouk and Rita Hayworth, to name but a few. No-one asks if you are anybody — it is presumed that you are!

During the six weeks of high season, Deauville is amiable, comfortable and unashamedly expensive! Built largely in the 1860s by the Duc de Morny, it has retained much of its original character as northern Europe's most elegant watering-place. Today it caters skilfully for a cosmopolitan influx of all tastes and pockets and its sporting and entertainment provision is legendary: La Touques racecourse, a sumptuous marina (Port Deauville) with moorings for over 900 craft, a polo ground, golf courses, tennis courts, swimming pools and much more besides. During the season there are gala nights and a number of festivals.

New building development is refreshingly tasteful, contrasting interestingly with neo-Gothic hotels and villas along Boulevard Eugène Cornuché — relics from the days when the monied classes brought their families and servants to summer here.

The course of the River Touques now takes us on the first of our excursions inland. The small town of the same name was once an important river-mouth port and still retains some old houses; summer exhibitions are held in the deconsecrated eleventh-century Église St Pierre. The remains of William the Conqueror's château at Bonneville-sur-Touques, however, are disappointingly meagre.

Pont-l'Évêque, a charming pays d'Auge town, straddles the busy N175 at an important crossroads and is close to the A13 Autoroute. Traffic apart, there are a number of old, dark half-timbered buildings to see, particularly at the west end in Rue St Michel, in Rue de Vaucelles and alongside the channelled River Yvie. The bridge after which the

town is named was built by a medieval bishop of Lisieux. World War II damage was considerable and much of the town's heritage was lost.

On Pont-l'Évêque's main street are several quaint old shops; those selling equestrian equipment are perhaps the most fascinating. Good car parking can be found by Église St Michel. As long ago as the thirteenth century, Pont-l'Évêque enjoyed a reputation for its fine cheeses and this continues to be the town's main distinction.

Glimpses of the River Touques' fertile east bank are gained in many places as the D579 rises and falls above the valley floor on its way south. Countryside around Pont-l'Évêque is characterised by *douets*, tributary streams of the Touques running through small villages and farms. A fine panorama of the Touques valley is gained from Pierrefitte-en-Auge, 5km south of Pont-l'Évêque on the D280. The little hilltop town of Beaumont-en-Auge, 6km west, also offers good views to the coast; it was the birthplace of the French mathematician Laplace.

Standing at the junction of the Touques and Orbiquet valleys, Lisieux is pays d'Auge's busiest commercial and market town. It is a matter of great regret that its old Gothic and Renaissance houses were destroyed in 1944, though a few isolated examples remain in Rue du Dr Lesigne, Rue Henry-Chéron and Rue P-Banaston.

Right at the centre, however, Cathédrale St Pierre escaped unscathed. Begun in 1170, it remained unfinished until the late 1200s. The exterior façade is raised above ground level on stone steps and is flanked by two towers. Walk round to the south transept to see the so-called 'Paradise Door', buttressed in the fifteenth century.

The cathedral's interior is strikingly elegant; massive round pillars support the nave's wide arches. It contains the tomb of Pierre Cauchon who became Bishop of Lisieux shortly after his betrayal of Joan of Arc and her

Born on 2 January 1873 into the wealthy
but very religious Martin family in
Alençon, Thérèse was brought to
Lisieux after her mother's death and
entered the Carmelite Order in April
1888, aged only 15. The life she had been
called to was solitary, hard and
profoundly spiritual, but she brought to
it an extraordinary directness, combined
with cheerfulness and driving energy.
Completing her life story — *History of a
Soul* — mere days before entering the
Carmelite Hospital with tuberculosis,
Sister Thérèse died in 1897, aged 24. Her
remains are enshrined in the Carmelite
Chapel and commemorated there in a
wax effigy dressed in the Order's coarse
brown habit.

subsequent execution by the English.
 Lisieux's renown today centres
around the short life of Ste Thérèse.

*Coupesarte manor-house*

Many locations in Lisieux are associated with Ste Thérèse, including Les Buissonnets, the family home, the cemetery in which she was buried, and displays depicting her life as a Carmelite in the north Cloister and at 57, Rue du Carmel.

The focal point for pilgrimages, especially notable on 15 August and the last Sunday in September, is a vast Romano-Byzantine basilica, begun in 1929 and consecrated in 1954. It stands a little way south-east out of town, its broad processional way and imposing dome (providing excellent views) floodlit on summer evenings. The mosaic-clad crypt contains more material on Ste Thérèse's life.

Elsewhere in the town is the Musée du Vieux Lisieux, with pays d'Auge pottery, old costumes and Gallo-Roman coins; as well as tennis courts, riding stables and a swimming pool.

Just to the south stands the huge, well-proportioned Château de Fervaques. Constructed during the sixteenth and seventeenth centuries from brick and stone, it typifies the manor-houses and castles to be found in this part of Normandy. (Only the exterior may be visited.)

20km south-east of Lisieux near the departmental borders with Eure and Orne, Orbec is a small market town with considerable character. There are several old houses in Rue Grande, as well as a fifteenth-century Hospice which sheltered plague victims. The medieval Église Notre-Dame is well worth seeing.

In meadows about 5km south, near la Folletière-Abenon, may be found the source of the River Orbiquet — a delightfully pastoral spot.

Pays d'Auge is well known for its lush pastures and the high quality of its dairy produce. Camembert has gained world-wide popularity and is often produced far from its place of origin. Three other famous cheeses — Pont-l'Évêque, Livarot and Pavé d'Auge — are produced in pays d'Auge from milk which derives its special flavour from the flora and climate of the region.

Manufacture of these cheeses is still restricted to the few villages around the centres whose names they carry. Livarot cheese, for example, has the distinction of having an *appellation d'origine,* one of only 20 French cheeses guaranteed to have been made within a defined area and using traditional methods. Until 1940, these pays d'Auge cheeses were made exclusively on farms and brought to local markets each week for sale to the finishers, or *cavistes,* who kept them in ripening rooms for three months before selling them to the general public. When regulations on the making of Livarot were imposed, including the use of only skimmed milk, farmers lost interest in its production and it is only in the past few decades that the cheese has been revived, made to the original recipe.

A Livarot of 600g takes 5 litres of milk. Curds are roughly chopped and put into moulds, drained, salted and cleaned before being placed in cellars to ripen on reed *glottes,* thus avoiding direct contact with the wooden shelves. Temperature and humidity are carefully controlled and a second fermentation occurs, until finally the cheese is bound with five strips of sedge and sold, about a hundred days after the milk came from the cow.

Livarot and other pays d'Auge cheeses should just yield to the touch and should be kept cool in a sealed box; open to room temperature four hours before eating.

A Route du Fromage is suggested — a circuit along narrow lanes through charming small pays d'Auge towns and past many picnic spots. From Livarot, take the D4 for St Pierre-sur-Dives, turning right on D273 to St Michel-de-Livet and le Mesnil-Durand; D43 to le Mesnil-Germain and Fervauqes; D64 to Notre-Dame-de-Courson and les Moutiers-Hubert; D110 to Bellou manor; D268 to Lisores; D579 to la Chapelle-Haute-Grue; and D155 via Heurtevent back to Livarot.

*French film crew in the showpiece village of Beuvron-en-Auge*

A museum dedicated to the life and work of the painter Ferdnand Léger is situated in a converted barn at Lisores.

Manoire de Coupesarte, 6km north-west of Livarot off the D45, lies up a rough track over a railway branch line. Discreet parking is called for, but viewing of this magnificent complex is allowed. The manor itself, standing amidst trees, is richly patterned with herringbone brickwork, half-timbering and little corner turrets — all reflected delightfully in a moat.

Back on the coast, the tour moves west from Deauville and Trouville along the Côte Fleurie to Cabourg. Blonville-sur-Mer and Benerville merge into one resort, united by a long, gently-shelving sandy beach which is ideal for children. A reconstructed Norman village on Mont Canisy just inland provides an interesting little diversion.

Beaches on this coast are truly vast, especially at low tide when dimensions seem infinite. At the end of a 5km stretch, Villers-sur-Mer clusters on its hillside like a pause at the end of a long sentence. Elegant, but less expensive and chic than Deauville, Villers nevertheless possesses all the ingredients for

*Château de Crèvecoeur-en-Auge*

holidaymaking and entertainment: sandy beaches, pleasant bars and restaurants, a casino, good shops and

scenic, wooded countryside to the south. Between Villers and Houlgate, the Auberville plateau ends abruptly in

---

### PLACES OF INTEREST IN PAYS D'AUGE

**Pont-l'Évêque**
Old shops and houses on busy crossroads.

**Château de Fervaques**
Typical sixteenth-century brick and stone château.

**Livarot**
Cheese-making centre on *Route du Fromage* circuit.

**Lisores**
Museum to painter Ferdnand Léger.

**Coupesarte Manor**
Unspoilt Manor and nearby Grandchamp Château.

**Beuvron-en-Auge**
Showpiece village typifying the Auge region.

**Château de Crèvecoeur-en-Auge**
Complex of picturesque buildings, museum of Norman architecture.

weathered, crumbling cliffs of dark clay and marl. They are eroded into ravines in places and rare fossils can be found in the lower clay strata, though it is about an hour's low-tide walk from the resorts at either end. Elsewhere along this dramatic edge of land, chalk cliffs have fallen away, seaweed-covered blocks forming the so-called *Vaches Noires* (Black Cows).

At Houlgate, cliffs give way to the Dives estuary and more popular, limitless sands. There is seafront parking with views west to the groynes and villas of Cabourg from the promenade; it reaches right to the cliff base and myriad rock pools. Predictably, views are even wider from the clifftops.

Houlgate seems to epitomise the Norman seaside resort — a charming, tree-shaded town in the green Drochon valley and a perfect base for exploring this part of the province, both coastal and inland. Amenities are generous too, including swimming pools with instruction, beach cabins, tennis courts, horse-riding, a 9-hole golf course, angling, walking and a casino. The town also contains a Fossil Museum and is host to a Music Festival.

Dives-sur-Mer saw the departure of one of the Middle Ages' most remarkable expeditions — Duke William's conquest of England. The main fleet assembled here, awaiting a favourable wind, until finally, on 12 September 1066, some 12,000 knights and foot soldiers set sail in 696 ships and an armada of smaller craft, calling at St Valery-sur-Somme for reinforcements. The full story is unfolded graphically in the famous tapestry at Bayeux.

Today, Dives lies almost 2km inland, its port silted up though there is a modern marina development near the River Dives' mouth. Linked closely with its sister resort of Cabourg, the town is both older and busier. Its massive Notre-Dame church is worth a visit, not least for a list of knights who accompanied William the Conqueror, which was carved on the back of the west wall in 1862.

150m to the north can be found the imposing timber roof of the Late Medieval Market Hall (*Halles*), still in good condition. There is a Craft Museum in the Hostellerie de Guillaume-le-Conquérant.

The River Dives meanders south for a considerable distance inland and by following it, the remainder of pays d'Auge and the country to the east of the Suisse Normande can be explored.

Quite close to the A13 Autoroute, Criqueville-en-Auge's sixteenth-century château boasts three main buildings and vast roofs. The hamlet is characteristically tiny, with a Commonwealth War Cemetery and much chequered brickwork. In fact, half-timbering and surface pattern is to be seen everywhere — a rich ornamentation adding more design to

---

## MAIN RESORTS ON THE CÔTE FLEURIE

**Blonville and Beneville**
Family beaches; reconstructed Norman village just inland on Mont Canisy.

**Villers-sur-Mer**
Lively resort; fossil hunting beneath cliffs, curious cliff-falls called *Vaches Noires* (Black Cows).

**Houlgate**
On River Dives estuary. Rock-pools and views from clifftop paths. Charming shady town with all amenities. Fossil museum.

**Dives-sur-Mer**
Whence William the Conqueror set sail for England in 1066. Medieval covered market hall, Craft Museum.

**Cabourg**
A quiet, genteel resort opposite Dives; vast sandy beaches at nearby Merville-Franceville-Plage.

the rows of trees and the shaping of fields already a feature of the landscape. Crucifixes stand tall and startlingly realistic, frequently life-size.

For the ultimate in showpiece villages, visit Beuvron-en-Auge, a protected site (*sauvegarde*) just to the south on D49 and full of brown-painted timberwork and tasteful little shops. Even its intimate back streets and private yards are lovingly cared for, though the result of all this lavish pride is a touch sanitised for lovers of the true vernacular.

Beuvron-en-Auge is close to the confluence of the rivers Dorette, Vie and Laizon, which merge uncertainly in a broad *marais* of marshy flats, especially around le Ham. Only by descending to this plain can one fully appreciate the elevated nature of the often wooded Côte d'Auge escarpment, running north-west from Lisieux to Cabourg and overlooking a great diversity of countryside. Pays d'Auge farms are often isolated in orchards (reminiscent of those in pays de Caux), their buildings containing oven, cider-press, apple stores and stables. The most favourable spot is reserved for the dairy. Elsewhere, undulating pastureland is interrupted by the prettiest of thatched cottages and grand old manor-houses.

Just of the N13 Lisieux to Caen road, from which it is half-obscured by foliage, stands a marvellously restored ensemble of eleventh to sixteenth-century buildings: Château de Crèvecoeur-en-Auge. Its highly decorative gatehouse entrance, by a large car park, leads to the château complex which houses a museum of Norman architecture. Substantially half-timbered outbuildings are surrounded by lawns, but an intriguing view of the main structure can be gained through a screen of trees and bushes near the road.

*Château de Falaise, birthplace of William the Conqueror*

*Statue of William the Conqueror, Falaise*

Some 12km south lies the busy little market town of St Pierre-sur-Dives, set in rich pastoral countryside. Rising above its rooftops, the thirteenth-century lantern tower of the warm-stoned old abbey church is all that remains of the reconstructed Benedictine abbey originally founded here at the instigation of William the Conqueror's aunt but subsequently burned down during conflicts between his sons. Its interior contains a *Grande Mosaique du Pays d'Auge.*

The same thirteenth-century monks also constructed the covered market (*Halles*) in Place du Marche. However, it was burned down in 1944 and painstakingly rebuilt in its original form using 290,000 chestnut pegs! Rather disappointing from the outside, a key may be obtained from the Café du Marché in the main square for viewing when the building is not in use. St Pierre also manufactures most of the boxes used to pack Normandy cheeses.

The River Dives now veers south-east

into Orne and attention turns to the valley of a tributary, the Ante. There are scattered rock spurs along its rugged course, an enduring medieval setting for one of Calvados' most appealing historic towns.

Falaise is a trim and spacious market town at the hub of incredibly straight radiating roads. New building is clean and mellow, shops are excellent and there is tennis, riding, swimming and camping in Val d'Ante beneath the town.

However, Falaise's great attraction — one for which it rightly prides itself — is its magnificent château. Built on the bedrock of an escarpment, it is one of Normandy's earliest stone castles, with a keep, a massive fifteenth-century round tower and 35m high flanking walls, 4m thick. The effect is almost fairy-tale and an impressive view may be gained from Promenade des Bercagnes, by the hospital.

Falaise was the birthplace of William the Conqueror, commemorated by a large and flamboyant statue in the cobbled Place Guillaume-le-Conquérant; William on horseback is flanked by the smaller figures of his first six dukes. Although the town suffered badly during World War II, this west quarter, containing most of interest, escaped damage. Even if its façade is in need of some attention, the Gothic Église La Trinité is worth a visit.

From the cobbled square, a steep slope leads into the château itself, wherein Duke William laid his plans for the invasion of England. The Great Hall's windows are original eleventh century, the dungeon is open to visitors and there is a memorial to William's companions at the Battle of Hastings in the St Poix chapel.

Falaise is a good centre for touring and walking in the nearby Suisse Normande and the whole town is imaginatively floodlit during the main summer season.

Another tributary of the Dives, the River Laizon, has hollowed out a gorge

---

---

through limestone crests, typical of the Falaise region. 9km north of the town, a steep path leads down to *Brèche au Diable* ('Devil's Breach'), a good example of this landscape feature.

Retracing our steps along the Dives towards the coast, we reach the small town of Troarn, not far east of Caen. Here lie the restored remains of Abbaye d'Ardenne, founded in the twelfth century, but ruinous by the nineteenth, and further damaged in World War II. The buildings now belong to institutes of agriculture. The nave of the thirteenth-century abbey church is pure Norman Gothic, while on the left of the first courtyard is a huge tithe barn.

Cabourg stands at the western end of the Côte Fleurie opposite Dives-sur-Mer, its origins as recent as 1860. Arranged in a fan-like semicircle, shady avenues radiate inland, lined with substantial villas and inviting gardens. Little has changed since the late 1800s and there is a distinct *fin de siècle* ambience, a reluctance to acknowledge the less gracious intrusions of twentieth-century life. Marcel Proust wrote *Within a Budding Grove* during a stay here, and much that he records is still recognisable.

The fulcrum of Cabourg's geometric

*Château de Caen*

plan is provided by the luxurious Grand
Hotel and Casino — huge white edifices
on the seafront, flanked behind by
colourful flower beds. Indeed, the entire
sea-wall promenade — Boulevard des
Anglais — is dwarfed by the hotel's
'palm court' façade, with its potted
plants and immaculately laid tables
glimpsed through plate glass.

There are many less ostentatious
hotels in the resort, and a good
scattering of shops, bars and bistros;
combined with a wide and open expanse
of beach, holidaymakers are well catered
for, though a restrained circumspection
tends to prevail.

A large marina has been established at
the river mouth, with its attendant
sailing school. Elsewhere, visitors will
find a swimming pool, an 18-hole golf
course, riding, tennis, horse-racing and a
daily summer market.

Towards the mouth of the River Orne,
sands at low tide are more extensive than
ever — almost 2km wide at Merville-
Franceville-Plage. Here, a unique
collection of intact World War II
German fortifications has been open to
the public since 1982 and is well worth
seeing. This is the first of many wartime
sites encountered on the Calvados coast
to the west.

Beaches from the Orne to the
Cotentin Peninsula were chosen for the
great D-Day Landings of June 1944.
Detailing these historic military
operations lies outside the scope of this
guide, but special reference is made to
visible remains and to the principal
memorials and museums.

First, however, an excursion inland
along the River Orne, broadest of the

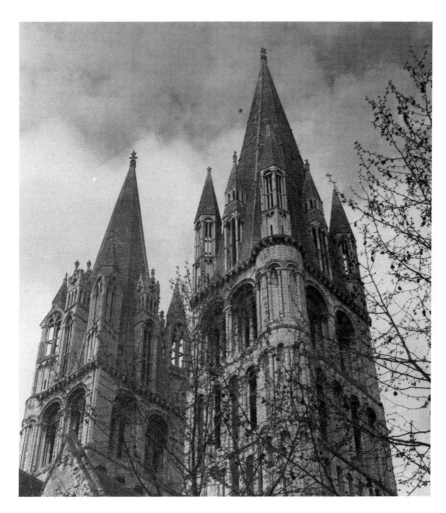

*Église St Pierre, Caen*

four river courses, culminating in the distinctive hill country of 'Suisse Normande'.

During the mid-1800s, a Baron Cachin initiated the excavation of a 12km-long canal parallel to the Orne between Caen and the sea. A series of locks was incorporated and Ouistreham made into an outer port: Caen's potential as a major seaport was thus greatly enhanced. Since its construction, the Caen canal has been repeatedly deepened and widened, with new basins added to accommodate ever-increasing traffic. Steel exports have been a major factor and ore barges of up to 16,000 tons laden, as well as ocean-going ships, are able to reach Caen.

Benouville, a hamlet on the canal with an eighteenth-century château, is best known for the Pegasus Bridge, a lifting steel structure spanning the canal. It was taken by the British 5th Paratroop Brigade after a brief engagement on the night of 5-6 June 1944, and there is a small museum. The bar opposite was the first house in France to be liberated by the Allies. Traffic is brought to a standstill during the passage of large ships and the bridge locality offers a fascinating vantage point.

Despite appalling war damage — two-thirds of the city was destroyed in June and July 1944 — Caen is still sometimes dubbed the 'Norman Athens'. Capital of Basse Normandie and chief town of Calvados, it is second only to Rouen as a major tourist centre in the province, with much to explore of artistic and antiquarian interest.

A good deal of what we see today is not true restoration, but skilful reconstruction in tranditional styles, so that the city, with its modern boulevards, its parks, gardens, waterways, squares and pedestrian precincts, is a more spacious, landscaped place than it once was. Its rebuilding, over fifteen years or so, ranks as one of France's great post-war successes. A distinguished and progressive city, it is one in which industriousness is complemented by leisure activity — there are more than a hundred sports centres alone! Caen University, founded by the English Duke of Bedford in 1432, is thriving, its new post-war campus to the north set out imaginatively over 80 acres.

Caen was a stronghold and favourite residence of William the Conqueror; while he was busy administering his new territory across the Channel, his wife Matilda was left in charge of the city. Duke William's citadel, erected in 1060 and added to in subsequent centuries, has been restored following war damage and is now laid out, both within the walls and outside, with delightful public gardens. Thanks to the clearance of surrounding buildings, the château's exceptionally fine curtain wall is clearly visible and there are fine views from its ramparts.

Contained within the château are two notable museums. The Musée des Beaux-Arts houses, in modern galleries, a wide range of works, from the Venetian and Flemish schools of the sixteenth and seventeenth centuries, through eighteenth-century French paintings, to nineteenth and early twentieth-century movements. There are also many decorative exhibits: enamels, porcelain, miniatures, gold and silver, furniture and tapestries. Engravings from an outstanding collection of over 50,000 are displayed in rotation.

---

PLACES OF INTEREST IN AND AROUND
CAEN

**Caen canal**
Links the city to the sea — many ships; Pegasus Bridge at Benouville.

**William the Conqueror's castle**
Rampart views, two fine museums: Fine Arts (paintings, engravings, decorative arts) and Normandy Folklore (farm life, costume, local handicrafts).

**Abbaye aux Dames**
Tomb of Mathilde, Duke William's wife; multi-columned crypt.

**Abbaye aux Hommes**
Duke William's tomb, many features of architectural interest.

**St Pierre**
Renaissance city merchants' church with high belfry.

Old houses and pedestrianised shopping precincts, numerous markets.

Dockside walks for views of shipping and River Orne.

*Maison des Quantrans, Caen*

---

The Musée de Normandie illustrates the province's folklore with material depicting the use of tools and utensils — on the farm (cheese and butter processing), women's costume (jewellery, head-dresses, etc) and local handicrafts (pottery, horse-harnesses, basketry, etc). Other nineteenth-century crafts such as pewter and brass ware, spinning, weaving and lace-making are found on the first floor, along with exhibits concerning religion, politics and folk art. There is also an Archaeology Hall.

Before leaving the château, look for the twelfth-century chapel which has become an impressive memorial to those who died in the battle for Caen in 1944.

Abbaye aux Dames, founded in 1042 by Queen Matilda, is one of two magnificent Romanesque abbeys in the city. The old buildings were reconstructed in the Classical style during the seventeenth century but suffered damage in World War II. La Trinité church was largely complete by the late eleventh century, but its spires were destroyed in the Hundred Years' War, robbing it of considerable elegance. Queen Matilda lies buried in the choir beneath a glass-edged slab. The crypt, which is marvellously preserved, may be visited to see its remarkable 'forest' of columns.

Prior to his becoming Archbishop of Canterbury, Abbot Lanfranc built the great Abbaye aux Hommes for William the Conqueror. Larger than Abbaye aux Dames to the east, its Église St Etienne and the abbey buildings form an historically and architecturally homogeneous complex. It was consecrated in 1077, 11 years after work had begun, though it was not completed until the thirteenth century. Badly damaged during the Wars of Religion and subsequently restored, it fortunately escaped harm in 1944. Duke William's tomb lies beneath a plain slab under the chancel arch before the high altar, though his remains were taken by the Huguenots in the sixteenth century and later thrown into the Orne during the Revolution.

The abbey's austere Romanesque gable façade is flanked by two tall and slender eleventh-century towers; while within may be found many interesting features, including beautiful seventeenth-century stalls. The adjacent Conventual Buildings, rich in carved woodwork, now accommodate the Hôtel-de-Ville but are open for guided tours. For a stunning view of the abbey, go to Place Louis-Guillouard, near the ruins of Église St Stephen.

It is interesting to recall that at the height of the battle for Caen, fires raged throughout the city for eleven days in June 1944, forcing residents to seek shelter in more substantial buildings: 1500 of them camped out in Abbaye aux Hommes.

Église St Pierre, parish church for city merchants, contrasts strikingly with the great abbey churches in its rich ornamentation. Particularly notable as an example of Renaissance architecture and decoration is the church's east end, built between 1518 and 1545. Capitals on pillars in the nave bear animal motifs and the five sixteenth-century apsidal chapels are finely vaulted, their carved keystones resembling stalactites.

St Pierre's original 78m high belfry, dating from 1308, was hit by a shell from HMS *Rodney* during the Battle of Caen and, in falling, damaged the nave. Reconstruction was carried out and the belfry is once again distinguished for its size.

In spite of wartime devastation, a few of Caen's old houses have survived, some examples being the Hôtel d'Escoville and 52 and 54, Rue St Pierre; and directly opposite the château's south wall, Maison des Quatrans. Isolated alongside the busy Rue Geôle, the latter is nevertheless an extraordinarily evocative structure.

Elsewhere in the city, modern buildings have been faced with mellow Oolitic limestone from the locality — stone which has weathered so well on the Tower of London and Canterbury Cathedral. Best of the pedestrianised shopping precincts are along Rue Froid, around Place de la République and in the Vaugeux quarter east of the château. There is a very pleasant Jardin des Plantes north-west of the centre, with good car parking along Fossés St Julien, while against a background of docks and basins, quay and riverside walks on the Orne offer views of Caen's shipping activities.

Markets are held on Fridays (St Sauveur), Sundays (St Pierre), Wednesdays and Saturdays (Cygne-de-Croix), Tuesdays and Thursdays (Chemin d'Anthie).

Caen is a popular destination; although the city and surrounding area are busy, they combine a wealth of sights and amenities with excellent positioning as a base from which to explore Calvados.

Not far south of Caen, the River Orne

*Le Tréport*

*Cricqueboeuf church, near Honfleur*

*The Vieux Bassin, Honfleur*

begins cutting through ancient rocks of the Armorican Massif which underlies this part of Normandy and extends its rugged influence west into Brittany. Between Thury-Harcourt and Putanges-Pont-Ecrepin, the Orne winds through gorges, wooded valleys and a jumble of steep sided hills. River bends have carved steep cliffs, often half-obscured by vegetation except at notable outcrops like Rocher du Parc, while here and there the topography rises to an isolated higher summit.

The French call this area 'Suisse Normande', though any resemblance to that most mountainous country farther east is a tenuous one indeed! Rather, the region consists of pretty, hilly countryside, verdant and agricultural, a good place for walkers, climbers, canoeists and anglers. In springtime, broom lights hillsides and riverbanks with an iridescent yellow and in autumn the woods are a riot of colour. It is worth driving on minor roads, following signed scenic routes — the views are delightful.

Thury-Harcourt, a popular resort town on the northern edge, is considered to be a gateway to Suisse Normande. Much rebuilt since 1944, its thirteenth-century church nevertheless retains its original façade. Less fortunate was the eighteenth-century château of the Dukes of Harcourt, burned to the ground; the ruins are now surrounded by a pleasant public park.

Thury-Harcourt is an excellent base for excursions along the Orne and to nearby places of interest. A signed

*Clécy, a touring centre in Suisse Normande*

*Château Pontécoulant*

---

motoring circuit through typical Suisse Normande countryside links the town with St Martin-de-Sallen, Culey-le-Patry, St Lambert, St Pierre-la-Vieille, Clécy, St Rémy, St Omer and Esson.

Mont Pinçon (365m), some 12km to the west, provides wide panoramas over the *bocage*. To reach it, turn along a rough track directly opposite a tall red and white TV mast (visible from afar). Passing other lesser aerials, proceed for about 500m and walk across scrubby heathland to find the best viewpoints.

Aunay-sur-Odon stands a little way north, a definitive example of reconstruction after almost total devastation during just three days of fighting in 1944. The spanking new town was rebuilt very quickly between 1947 and 1950, its huge slate-roofed church completed by 1958.

Roads flank the River Orne south from Thury-Harcourt, but at Pont-de-la-Mousse only the long-distance footpath, GR36, continues on the west bank, the D562 continuing along the east bank to St Rémy. Ironworks here were operational from 1875 to 1967, producing Normandy's richest ore and even today, what remains of the old mining installations are stained ochre-red. There is a good view of the Orne valley from the cemetery of a small restored church on a hilltop 700m from the main road.

Often dubbed the capital of Suisse Normande, Clécy is in season a tourist hub for walkers, climbers and anglers (although it is a small place and with limited accommodation). This is highly picturesque country and there are several waymarked walks, of one to three hours' duration, to local beauty spots. These include *Pain de Sucre* (Sugar Loaf) for wide views of the Orne, reached via the little church at Vey hamlet; the 260m high l'Éminence viewpoint; and la Croix de la Faverie. The 10km *Route des Crêtes* drive also takes in many of these features. Details may be obtained from the town's *Syndicat d'Initiative*.

1 km east is Pont du Vey, with its old mill (now an inn) and great splashing waterwheels. Clécy's sixteenth-century Manoir de Placy houses an interesting antiques and local crafts museum: entry tickets include free cider tasting. A miniature railway and associated museum in the park will be of special appeal to children and enthusiasts.

Condé-sur-Noireau lies at the border with Orne department, another substantially rebuilt township, but with two interesting churches. The restored St Sauveur boasts a remarkable timber vault, St Martin a thirteenth-century choir.

Nearby Château Pontécoulant, a smart state-run building dating back three centuries, is set in a landscaped park close to a fishing lake. Its interior is now a museum and contains much fine old furniture.

Passing high escarpments, the River Noireau leads back through Pont-Erambourg to its confluence with the Orne at Pont-d'Ouilly, a crossroads and touring base. After a brief coincidence with the departmental border, the River Orne enters the Gorges St Aubert and leaves Calvados. It has been followed inland from the Channel and it is time to return there and explore the coast and hinterland to the west.

From the lighthouse and shipping control tower at the entrance to the Caen Canal, Ouistreham-Riva-Bella stretches round the easternmost corner of the *Côte de Nacre* ('Mother of Pearl Coast'). It is a sprawling community: part town, part fishing port, part international yachting centre, part residential; an altogether larger settlement than others on this coast.

Riva-Bella contains the holidaymaking elements — go-karting, pony-rides, casino, funfairs and *frites* — and has excellent sands backed by clusters of pale wooden beach huts along low dunes. Ouistreham's much restored twelfth-century church, with a

---

### PLACES OF INTEREST IN 'SUISSE NORMANDE'

**Thury-Harcourt**
Gateway to the region, pleasant town and park; start of signed circular tour of Suisse Normande for motorists and cyclists.

**Mount Pinçon**
Wide panoramas over the *bocage*.

**Clécy**
Touring centre for walkers, anglers, cyclists, etc. Delightful small town; local walks to viewpoints and beauty spots.

**Manoir de Placy**
Antiques and local crafts museum at sixteenth-century manor; also miniature railway in park.

**Château Pontécoulant**
Fishing lake and interior museum with fine furniture.

---

magnificent gabled façade, was built as a fortress against English raiders: in much more recent times, the whole town was one of the first to be liberated in 1944.

A commemorative Museum of the Normandy Landings has been established, though outside all that remains of the war is a lone blockhouse on the north shore. Anglo-French Commandos landed on this section of the coast — known as Sword Beach and open to German long-range guns at Le Havre — linking with airborne troops at Pegasus Bridge in advance of the British 3rd Division. The commander of the British forces was honoured at Colleville-Montgomery-Plage by inclusion of his name and the erection of a statue. In an effort to form a crude breakwater and protect Sword Beach during the Landings, the old French battleship *Courbet* was sunk off la Brèche-d'Hermanville.

*Remains of the Mulberry Harbour, Arromanches*

Today, semi-urban ribbon development runs frieze-like above a succession of sandy beaches, past Lion-sur-Mer with its twelfth-century largely Romanesque church and private château to the conspicuous white casino at Luc-sur-Mer. The sea-air at this pleasant resort is especially bracing and there is a spa offering sea-water cures. The Parc Municipal, an oasis of luxuriant plants and trees, provides a refreshing counterpoint to seaside amenities.

Langrune-sur-Mer is said to derive its name from the Scandinavian *Land-grun,* a name also given to Greenland: the most likely reference is to banks of green seaweed exposed at low tide. It is a small, rather undistinguished resort, with a generous complement of hotels, guest houses and cafés. The beautiful two-storey belfry of its thirteenth-century church is reputedly copied from that of St Etienne in Caen.

2km to the south, across the flat Caen countryside, rise the tall spires of Notre-Dame-de-la-Délivrande, scene of bitter fighting to eliminate German artillery spotters on D-Day. A much venerated Black Madonna is contained within the nineteenth-century Neo-Gothic Basilica

and major pilgrimages take place on 15 August, the following Thursday and 8 September.

First to be mentioned of many in the region bearing the war dead of America, Britain, Canada, Germany and Poland, the military cemetery at Douvres-la-Délivrande contains almost 1000 British graves. Some, like this one, are small, shady and intimate; others are overwhelming in their size and ability to evoke the tragic loss of life which occurred here during World War II. La Cambe German War Cemetery, between Bayeaux and Isigny, has the sad distinction of holding the greatest number of graves — over 21,000.

St Aubin-sur-Mer exudes an authentic, unspoilt charm, differentiating it from neighbouring resorts — this is holidaymaking land, with amenities and beaches tending to merge along the coastal strip. St Bernières-sur-Mer's thirteenth-century church is notable for a 3-level stone spire reaching a height of 67m; inside are Romanesque nave and aisles, though the vaulting is reconstructed, and a seventeenth-century stone altarpiece. The restored headquarters of a French-

Canadian infantry regiment in the town is also worth a visit.

Famous for its Breton and Portuguese oysters, brought here from the Ile de Ré to mature in special beds, Courseulles-sur-Mer is a fast-developing holiday town, with a fishing harbour, marina, swimming pool, tennis courts and many other sporting facilities. However, in common with much of this popular coast, it has become vulgarised by insensitive new buildings. Huge wedges of apartments dwarf their surroundings, especially near the port, and although lip-service is paid to the use of traditional materials — slate roofs and cladding, with muted colours — the effect is unmistakably high-rise or tower-block. It may make sense as far as economics are concerned, but this once-quiet resort has paid a high price in terms of the ugliness of its landscape and the fact that its character has been irreversibly altered.

Courseulles is situated in the Canadian sector of Juno Beach at the time of the Allied Invasion of June 1944. A commemorative Sherman tank, reclaimed from the sea in 1971, now dominates the town's central square.

The predominantly flat shoreline is echoed in open farmlands around Caen, but farther west, undulating pastures and a tight matrix of villages and interconnecting lanes hold much of interest for the visitor. The scars of war have healed. Damaged towns are carefully restored, the imprint of fighting lost beneath the plough and decades of vegetation, the people preoccupied with farming and fishing.

South of Courseulles in delightful wooded countryside stands a most handsome Renaissance château. Fontaine-Henry is a quite outstandingly graceful, almost regal, edifice with some of the highest slate roofs in France, one taller than the building which it surmounts. Erected on the site of a thirteenth-century keep, its detailed stonework and interior clearly show the transition from late fifteenth-century Gothic ornamentation to sixteenth-century Classical style.

The château has not changed hands and is a lived-in 'stately home'; visiting hours are posted at the entrance in the charming little Place du Château outside the perimeter fence. The interior is magnificently furnished with many antiques, there is an especially fine sixteenth-century staircase, as well as various sculptures and a very good collection of paintings by Poussin, Regaud and others.

The gem of a twelfth-century Romanesque church at the busy little hamlet of Thaon is deconsecrated and unused, but is worth seeing for its original belfry with pyramidal roof and deep bays.

Still a very fine building (now a horticultural training college), the former priory of St Gabriel-Brécy was founded in the eleventh century and was a dependency of Fécamp Abbey. South of the village stands Château Brécy, surrounded by marvellous terraced gardens with topiary and wide views.

Back on the coast, a rash of caravans, chalets and beach-huts lead west past Vers-sur-Mer, with its massive Romanesque church, until the land rises at St Côme-de-Fresne. This popular stopping point for motorists provides an excellent panorama over the remains of one of the two great 'Mulberry Harbours'. Visitors often find it surprising that so many components of this vast artificial dock are still visible (particularly the offshore breakwaters), having survived over forty years of sea erosion. There is a lookout tower with telescopes, summer helicopter trips and a monumental white Madonna overseeing all. Families with young children are warned that the cliff edge is dangerous, as it is subject to crumbling.

Arromanches-les-Bains was known only to a few discriminating French families who loved its spacious beach before the events of 1944 etched its name into history. On 7 June, four thousand ships and a thousand smaller craft landed the Allied armies within the shelter of 'Mulberry B' harbour (known to the French as Port Winston). The harbour area, larger than Dover, was equipped with floating pontoons that enabled troops to land at any state of the tide. It was a feat without precedent and on a scale which has never been equalled.

A rather severe concrete building, the principal Landings Museum is easily located at the east end of Arromanches. The exhibition it houses is impressive and includes Royal Navy and American film, weapons, uniforms, photographs, plans and maps, autographs and dioramas. Artillery pieces are on display outside and beached pier supports are accessible at low tide.

In high season, milling crowds admitted in guided groups conspire against a thoughtful appreciation of the material, but a visit is well worth while nevertheless. The Museum is open all year and, with all the beaches on which landings took place, is perhaps best seen out of season when swimsuited holidaymakers and brilliant sunshine are no longer uneasily juxtaposed with the sober relics of war.

Before exploring the last stretch of coastline to the Vire estuary, a short, almost obligatory, detour inland should be made to Bayeux, historic town par excellence and guardian of the great Bayeux tapestry (*Tapisserie de la Reine Mathilde*).

Originally intended as a cathedral wall-hanging, this band of wool-embroidered linen, 70m long, depicting decisions and events which determined the history of England as much as Normandy, is now housed in its own museum — the Centre de Guillaume-le-

---

PLACES OF INTEREST ON THE CALVADOS COAST

**Ouistreham-Riva-Bella**
Good sands and holiday amenities; Museum of Normandy Landings.

**Luc-sur-Mer**
Sea-water cures, luxuriant park.

**Douvres-la-Délivrande**
British Military Cemetery.

**Couseulles-sur-Mer**
Famous for oysters. Holiday town with fishing harbour, marina and many sports. Commemorative town-centre Sherman tank.

**Château de Fontaine-Henry**
Stately home, inland, with magnificent interior and exterior.

**Arromanches-les-Bains**
Impressive principal Landings Museum. Views of World War II 'Mulberry Harbour' remains.

**Port-en-Bessin**
Small fishing port with fish auctions and colourful craft along quaysides. Coastal views from outer jetties.

**St Laurent-sur-Mer**
Main American Military Cemetery: over 9000 graves, central memorial, beautifully tended.

**Vierville-sur-Mer**
World War II museums, here and at Surrain (5km inland).

**Pointe du Hoc**
Untouched battlefield as living memorial to Landings; bunkers, shell-holes, gun emplacements.

**Grandchamp-Maisy**
Fishing boats and holiday town with good views west.

*Rue St Martin, Bayeux*

Conquérant. It is imaginatively presented, with great clarity, taste and care. An introductory multi-screeen, impressionistic slide-show is followed by viewing a replica of the tapestry (bearing explanatory notes in French and English) and a short film. The tapestry proper occupies three sides of a rectangle, with optional commentary available in English from portable earpieces hired on entry. Books, slides, postcards, etc can be purchased at the exit and visitors will find the whole show both educational and entertaining.

Bayeux was the first major town to be liberated by the advancing Allies in 1944 and thus, having escaped significant damage, remains a place of splendid old buildings and quaint shopping streets — a paradise for people who like to explore such towns in a leisurely fashion. Try walking, for example, from the Dean's house near the Cathedral to the eighteenth-century Bishopric, down Rue des Cuisiniers to Rue St Martin and thence along Rue St Malo, Rue Franche and back along Rue Bienvenue.

An old-established, former Roman community and a bishopric since the fourth century, Bayeux is best known as the cradle of the Norman Dukedom. Rollo the Viking, first Duke of Normandy, married Popa, daughter of Bayeux's Governor in AD 904. Their son was to become known as William Longsword, ancestor of William the Conqueror, and subsequent events gave Bayeux its central place in Normandy's history at that time.

Cathédrale Notre-Dame is stunning — a glorious, typically Gothic structure built between 1050 and 1077. The two Romanesque towers of the façade were later buttressed to support their spires; the central tower is fifteenth century, though the top, the so-called *bonnet,* was rebuilt in the nineteenth century.

Tall windows and vaulting inside are

*Cathédrale Notre-Dame, Bayeux*

thirteenth century, while twelfth-century arches show the characteristic Norman Romanesque carving for which they are noted. There is a treasury, an eleventh-century crypt and a beautiful twelfth-century Gothic Chapter House. Best views of the exterior are from the street behind Passage Flachat, by the west door. The cathedral is floodlit during the summer season.

Bayeux was, and still is, a small lace-making centre and examples may be found in the Musée Baron-Géard in the Bishop's Palace, across a square dominated by a 'Liberty' plane tree planted in 1797. The museum houses Impressionist paintings, porcelain, old and modern Bayeux lace and Rouen ceramics, as well as woodwork, local paintings, and those by Flemish and Italian sixteenth-century 'primitives'.

Close to the British Military Cemetery on Boulevard Fabian Ware, a recently opened museum to the Battle for

Normandy records events during June and July 1944.

Saturday markets are held in Place St Patrice, there are some botanical gardens and a variety of leisure amenities. It is worth bearing in mind, however, that Bayeux has become a cosmopolitan tourist centre and in high season suffers, like all such places, from a pressing stream of visitors and traffic.

Standing on the coast between the beaches which during the Normandy landings were code-named Omaha and Gold, Port-en-Bessin was itself originally planned as a naval base in the seventeenth century. Its large outer harbour is protected by two long, semi-circular jetties from which there are excellent views of tall and often crumbling marl cliffs — from Cap Manvieux in the east to Pointe Percée in the west.

Though also a modest seaside resort, Port-en-Bessin is primarily a working port with a fish auction each Monday, Wednesday and Thursday. Fishing vessels will be seen lining the quaysides — a chaos of masts and rigging, brightly coloured paintwork, nets and rusting winches. It is a fascinating scene, well worth a leisurely stroll round. A couple of smart bars on the harbour front beyond the lock gates are the only real concession to tourism, but this adds to, rather than detracts from, the little port's appeal.

Not far to the west, between Colleville-sur-Mer and St Laurent-sur-Mer, lies the principal American Military Cemetery. Despite the passage of many thousands of visitors each year, the grounds are kept immaculate and a sense of quiet reverence prevails. Maps of the invasion strategy, as well as World War II's course farther afield, appear on a central memorial near a monumental bronze figure. All around, radiating across acres of mown grass, lie 9,386 graves, each marked by a white marble headstone cross or Star of David. Individual servicemen's names on each tomb lend an almost unbearable

poignancy to an already moving place. Saddest of all, perhaps, are the graves of those 'Known only to God'.

There are more monuments to the landings at both ends of the sea-wall road at les Moulins and at Vierville-sur-Mer where there also stands the commemorative Musée Omaha — American exhibits in a Nissen hut. Another collection of particularly fine material and rare mementos can be found in the Musée de la Libération de Normandie at Surrain, 5km south of St Laurent.

Relics of World War II are visible from place to place across much of Normandy, though farming has long since raked away the actual scars of battle. Vegetation and ceaseless erosion by weather and waves have obscured much, and the land has healed, the visible remnants of bitter conflict all but absorbed by the earth itself.

There is, however, one contrived exception to this natural process — a deliberate baring of a wound so that we shall not forget the horror that caused it: Pointe du Hoc. Here, shell-holes, gun

PLACES OF INTEREST IN BAYEUX

**Bayeux Tapestry**
Housed in special museum with audio-visual shows, commentaries, etc.

**Baron-Gérard Museum**
Impressionist paintings, porcelain, Bayeux lace, ceramics and much else.

**Cathédrale Notre-Dame**
Magnificent eleventh-century edifice, much of interest inside and out.

**British Military Cemetery**

**Museum to Battle of Normandy**

Quaint shopping streets and many old buildings.

emplacements and bunkers remain untouched, a covering of grass the only cosmetic masking of battlefield mud.

Using rope ladders, the American 2nd Rangers Batallion scaled these great crumbling yellow cliffs held by a strategic German position which posed a severe threat to troops landing on Omaha Beach below. Out on the point, a granite stele with inscribed plaques in French and English remembers their courage. Beneath the stele, in a warren of concrete rooms, are the names of some who perished and a chilling view of the sea through a gun-slit.

Access and pathways were improved for the Fortieth Anniversary celebrations, yet the site remains steadfastly undeveloped. Only a scatter of fellow sightseers stands between oneself and a vivid picture of those historic days in June 1944.

Grandchamp-Maisy, at the west end of Omaha Beach, has been much promoted as a holiday resort, but its old port still harbours a small fleet of fishing boats. Its thirteenth-century church is worthy of inspection and there are good views west across the Baie des Veys to the Cotentin Peninsula.

The small agricultural town of Isigny-sur-Mer has lost its seaside to

encroaching silt at the mouth of the River Vire. By way of consolation, however, the rich surrounding alluvial pastures are grazed by cattle whose milk gives world-famous dairy produce. It goes to the Isigny butter co-operative and the main dairy plant is open to visits. Isigny's attractive Hôtel-de-Ville was once a seventeenth-century château, home of the Bricqueville family until 1821.

We are at the departmental border with Manche, for a while shadowed inland by the River Vire, until the border itself turns in a zigzagging easterly loop to the Forêt de Cerisy.

9km east, near the main Bayeux to St Lô road, stands the Château de Balleroy, its gravel drive prolonging the curiously wide main street of Balleroy village (the D73 road). Grounds designed by le Nôtre are considered to be a masterpiece of the landscape gardener's art -- a blend of low walls, lawns and hedges and magnificent flower borders, all adding to a sense of symmetry and order created by the château's austere classical façade and its huge blue and gold decorative iron entrance gates.

Owned by the American Advisory Institute, the unique Musée des Ballons (housed in an outbuilding on the left) contains exhibits from Montgolfier's day to the present and is the venue for an annual gathering of balloonists from many countries.

Château de Balleroy was planned by François Mansart, Louis XIII's master architect, and was put up between 1626 and 1636. The opulence of its interior is not hinted at from outside. Painted ceilings, fine furniture and remarkable portraits bombard the visitor's eye, and there is a large library too.

Shops selling ceramics line the D572 just north of Balleroy — a cottage industry churning out endless urns, pots, garden furniture and echelons of statuettes which stand shamelessly naked and white, frozen in classical posture!

---

PLACES OF INTEREST IN WESTERN CALVADOS

**Château de Balleroy**
Landscaped gardens, Ballooning Museum, opulent interior.

**Pottery shops and studios**
Along D572 road north of Balleroy around le Tronquay and Noron-la-Poterie.

**Vire**
Eighth-century fortress town on escarpment above forest, river and ravines. Twelfth-century church, public gardens and reconstructed Norman farmhouse.

---

*Château de Balleroy*

Country to the south and east seems less picturesque. The heavy monotone of slate appears more widely and barns are roofed with that economical but visually distasteful substitute for traditional materials — corrugated iron. Hilltop Caumont-l'Eventé's slender church tower contrasts incongruously with that of neighbouring Cahagnes, a modernistic monstrosity like some huge electricity sub-station.

In the south-west corner of Calvados, we rejoin the River Vire at the town of the same name. Built rather like an amphitheatre on its escarpment, and a fortress town since the eighth century, Vire overlooks forests, rivers and deep ravines. It has long been an important crossroads between Brittany and eastern Normandy and its strategic position led to its virtual obliteration in World War II.

Today's town, bright and mostly new, acts as a market for dairy herds in the close-knit *bocage,* a region of small fields enclosed by banks and hedges. Though much of old Vire sadly disappeared in World War II, some ancient buildings remain and the people of Calvados are justly proud of this historic place. Main access is still through the splendid fortified Port-Horloge, with its added fifteenth-century tower. Although the town's twelfth-century château has mostly gone, there is a pleasant walk from its two remaining towers to the Rocher des Ranes viewpoint above the confluence of the Vire and Virenne. Their valleys are collectively known as the 'Vaux de Vire', which became associated with a local fifteenth-century clothmaker's bawdy tavern songs: rumour has it that the term 'vaudeville' was thus born.

Vire's twelfth-century Église Notre-Dame and the Jardin Public are both worth visiting, the latter for a reconstructed Norman farmhouse in the grounds of the medieval Hôtel-Dieu. Markets are held each Friday and there are facilities for swimming, riding and tennis.

# 5 Manche

The Cotentin Peninsula juts out squarely and points a finger at Lyme Bay in Dorset: this is northern Manche, unequivocally maritime with a breath of Brittany on the wind. Its rugged granite coast dips gently down to the east in rocky reefs, punctuated by the delightful fishing harbours of St Vaast-la-Hougue and Barfleur. Beyond the bustling Atlantic port of Cherbourg, the same granite rises to form the wild and remote Nez de Jobourg and Cap de la Hague whose gorse-covered moorland and cliff promontories are fully exposed to the moods of sea and weather.

Manche's long western seaboard contains some of France's remotest beaches and is generously washed by an arm of the Gulf Stream, endowing it with a subtly warmer climate. Popular resorts there are, but between them lie smaller settlements, while river estuaries and cliffs alternate with endless sands.

Utah Beach runs above the Vire estuary in the east. Flat marshes inland formed a major drop-zone for American airborne troops on D-Day and today the area bears numerous memorials and museums commemorating June 1944.

Although much was destroyed during World War II, much still remains or has been carefully restored, ensuring that the character of individual settlements is retained: lovers of architecture will not be disappointed. Fine buildings will be found in both historic towns and in lonelier settings, most famous of all the abbey-fortress of Mont-St-Michel at the peninsula's foot on Brittany's border.

Manche is a *département* of great diversity. Many consider it to be the best introduction of all to Normandy, a region in which the visitor can wander well off the beaten track, discovering intimate details of a single area, or tour round the network of rural lanes from one sleepy village to the next.

By drawing an imaginary line across alluvial flatlands from Carentan to Lessay, Manche is divided into two. If the sea level were to rise a dozen or more metres, this division would become a reality. The tour of Manche begins with its northern half, bounded by sea on three sides and leading to some of the least frequented parts of Normandy.

Carentan, with neighbouring Isigny-sur-Mer, is a major dairy market town whose port is now silted up with alluvial deposits from the converging rivers Vire, Taute and Douve. Its massive fourteenth-century Église Notre-Dame is one of the finest Gothic churches in the whole of Normandy, dominating the skyline with its octagonal-spired belfry.

These flood-prone flatlands across the neck of the peninsula are known as the 'Cotentin Pass'. Dairy cattle and horses (for which the region is renowned) graze open pastures, while human settlements have sought out low hills or the alluvial plateau around Ste Mère-Église on which to become established. The landscape is low and level, relieved only by lines of willow, dark clusters of cattle and occasional wildfowl.

In recent years, peat-cutting has brought new vigour to Baupte, a small town in the marshy centre of this lower plain. Over 70,000 tons annually are taken for use as fuel to generate electricity and in the manufacture of fertilisers. A nearby seaweed processing plant extracts valuable industrial colloids required by the plastics industry.

Ste Marie-du-Mont, on the D913 north of Carentan, possesses a fine Landings Museum, sometimes manned by local youngsters. There is also a

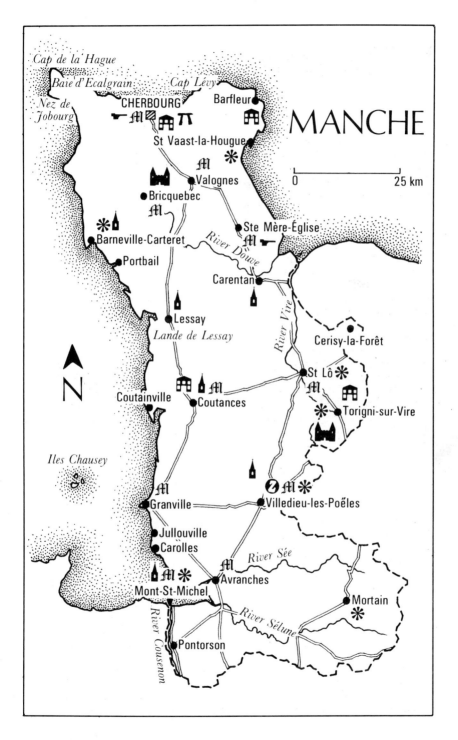

MANCHE

Cap de la Hague

Baie d'Ecalgrain

Cap Lévy

Nez de Jobourg

CHERBOURG

Barfleur

St Vaast-la-Hougue

Valognes

Bricquebec

Ste Mère-Église

Barneville-Carteret

Portbail

River Douve

Carentan

Lessay

Lande de Lessay

Cerisy-la-Forêt

River Vire

St Lô

Coutainville

Coutances

Torigni-sur-Vire

Iles Chausey

Granville

Villedieu-les-Poêles

Jullouville

Carolles

River Sée

Mont-St-Michel

Avranches

Mortain

River Sélune

River Couesnon

Pontorson

0          25 km

N

*Memorial to American Paratroopers of World War II, Ste Mère-Église*

monument here to the 4th Division American Infantry who landed nearby on Utah Beach, most westerly in the American sector. Ste Marie's fourteenth-century church is also worth seeing.

At la Madeleine, on the dune-backed coast, stand several monuments, a 'Liberty Way' marker stone, and a memorial crypt. A rose-granite, prow-like stele at les-Dunes-de-Varreville remembers the 2nd French Armoured Division.

First of the symbolic 'Liberty Way' marker stones on the so-called 'Liberty Highway' from Ste Mère-Église right across northern France to Metz, can be found in front of the Hôtel-de-Ville. It is number '0' and subsequent marker stones were placed at 1km intervals.

Ste Mère-Église, a town made famous by the film *The Longest Day* and first to be liberated by the United States forces, is still a venue for American war veterans on 6 June each year. Its town-centre church became a focus of fighting as American Paratroops came under fire from snipers in the tower: it is visibly pock-marked and a lifelike commemorative effigy of a paratrooper hangs by his harness from the balustrade. The story is further celebrated in a modern stained glass window.

Beneath a roof domed like a parachute in adjacent parkland, the

Airborne Troops Museum holds many fascinating exhibits from the events surrounding D-Day. There are weapons, models, maps, documents, even aircraft, and some of the best military photographs from the war. Indeed, the little town seems dedicated still to the memory of liberation, postcards of troops and battle displacing the more usual anodyne views. Considering the volume of inquisitive visitors it receives, this odd sense of time-warp is altogether understandable.

Except between les Grougins and Quinéville, sand-dunes obscure views of the sea from the coast road. An ugly miscellany of beach houses, small settlements and old gun positions sprawl northwards. Telegraph wires sag untidily from one ugly concrete post to the next — a visual blight common to many parts of rural France.

At high water, the sea rides startlingly high against the land. The Cotentin's north-east edge — Val de Saire — is a granite plateau sloping gently beneath the waves. Its lack of height, however, is misleading, for this is a rugged, threatening coast of broken reefs and treacherous currents. The sea is held uneasily at bay behind walls and dykes.

Inland of this coastal fringe, impressions change. Towns, villages and low hills were thought by John Ruskin in the mid-nineteenth century to resemble Worcestershire and certainly there is often a resemblance to that most English county. Were it not for sea to the north, east and west, similarities might have been more profound.

Valognes specialises in the manufacture and sale of dairy foods, particularly butter. Severe war damage resulted in wholesale reconstruction, and although a few substantial old houses still stand, the town is an undistinguished modern one. Nevertheless, there are two recommended ports of call: Maison Beaumont, open during the summer, is an impressive building with a 50m long façade overlooking terraced gardens;

---

## WORLD WAR II MEMORIALS AND MUSEUMS IN THE COTENTIN PENINSULA

### Ste Marie-du-Mont
Landings Museum and monument on Utah Beach.

### La Madeleine
Several monuments and memorial crypt.

### Ste Mère-Église
First 'Liberty Way' marker stone; shell-pocked church with commemorative Paratrooper effigy; Airborne Troops Museum with weapons, models, maps, photographs, aircraft, etc.

### Cherbourg
Liberation Museum in hilltop Fort du Roule.

and the Musée du Cidre in the fifteenth-century Logis de Grand Quartier illustrates stages in the cider-making process.

A busy fishing and yachting centre, St Vaast-la-Hougue faces south towards Utah Beach. Incoming craft are said to be guided by the white-painted apse of a little eleventh-century fishermen's chapel at the harbour's east end, though this depends upon it receiving an occasional lick of paint! The harbour itself dries out completely at low tide.

There are superlative views of surrounding reefs and islets from the 400m long granite jetty with its lighthouse. It is possible to walk across to the sizeable Ile de Tatihou at low water, with obvious care needed over timing the return.

The isthmus causeway to the fortified island of La Hougue is flanked by 2km of sand — the Grande Plage. Vauban's seventeeth-century Fort de la Hougue

squats impassively at the end and there is an interesting walk round its granite walls.

St Vaast is an absorbing place in which to wander. Fishing boats and yachts come and go on the tide, while local mariners in ubiquitous blue smocks go about their business weighing catches, boatbuilding, mending nets and bringing in oysters (which are cheap, plentiful and very good here) by tractor. There are several bars and restaurants on the quaysides, though one or two seem to be the exclusive domain of local fishermen.

Quettehou has good sea views, especially from its church cemetery, and is a useful centre for walks in the dense woodlands and pretty rolling countryside of Val de Saire. From a German blockhouse beyond the rebuilt church at nearby la Pernelle, there is a magnificent panorama in clear weather, stretching from Pointe Percée in the

*St Vaast-la-Hougue*

*Boatbuilding at St Vaast-la-Hougue*

south-east to the Gatteville lighthouse in the north.

Flat fields of cabbage, carrots and the covered heads of flax are protected from the sea by dykes reminiscent of the Low Countries. Farmsteads and manor-houses, often astonishingly grandiose, are encountered quite unexpectedly in hamlets or set back from the road. One such is the fortified Manoir de Crassvillerie, a handsomely-proportioned, grey-stone building on the little D1 coast road.

Heavy granite houses roofed with slate echo the austere, phlegmatic ambience that pervades the once-famous fishing port of Barfleur. Quieter and less visited than St Vaast, it will appeal to lovers of peaceful places where the pace of life is slowed. Even here, however, an increasing number of pleasure craft owners are discovering the attractions of its large, unspoilt harbour; in the summer season Barfleur is pleasantly animated.

Montfarville church to the south repays a visit, as will the conspicuous Phare de la Pointe de Barfleur (Gatteville lighthouse) — at 71m high, one of the tallest in France. Its light is

*Repairing nets at St Vaast-la-Hougue*

visible from a distance of 56km and, in conjunction with its radio beacon, guides ships into Le Havre. There is a vast coastal panorama from the top, and the granite Saire tableland can be seen dipping east into the sea.

Offshore waters are shallow, currents swift. The famous 'White Ship' carrying William Atheling, son of Henry I, sank hereabouts, drowning the heir to the English throne and all his 300 companions.

Although he spent little time there, the Château de Tocqueville was once the home of the scientist, social historian and liberal, Alexis de Tocqueville (1805-59). The original twelfth-century château fort has mostly disappeared, the present building dating from the eighteenth century.

A 228km long-distance footpath (GR223, *Sentier Tour du Cotentin*) starts from St Vaast or Barfleur, leading right round the coast to Avranches — a splendid hike for the keen long-distance walker. A short variant across Val de Saire from St Vaast to Cap Lévy would make a fine two-day trip.

The miniature port of Fermanville provides scenic access to Cap Lévy. Low, gorse-covered cliffs lead out to the modern grey lighthouse with good views east across the Anse (Bay) de la Mondrée. The delightful D116 corniche road continues west past the Pointe du Brulay viewpoint and little Anse de Brick.

At Bretteville, take a left turn (D320) on a narrow lane to see a 4000-year-old burial place (*Allée Couverte*) — a double row of upright stones supporting horizontal slabs to form a covered tunnel. The site is unsigned and needs to be watched for on the left before the main D901 is reached near Maupertus airport.

*The harbour, Barfleur*

The Renaissance Château de Tourlaville stands south of the village in parkland containing exotic plants, beech trees and ponds: access on foot from the crossroads triangle.

Almost an outskirt of Cherbourg, the

---

### PLACES OF INTEREST ON THE COAST EAST OF CHERBOURG

**St Vaast-la-Hougue**
Busy fishing port and yachting centre; walk to Ile de Tatihou or along Grande Plage to Vaubans's fortified La Hougue island; good cheap oysters.

**Quettehou**
Fine sea views from la Pernelle German blockhouse; wooded walks inland in Val de Saire.

**Manoir de Crassvillerie**
Farm on D1 coast road.

**Barfleur**
Large peaceful harbour; Montfarville church; Gatteville lighthouse, one of the tallest in France.

**Cap Lévy**
Gorse-covered cliffs and coastal views.

**'Allée Couverte'**
4000 year-old burial chamber.

little elongated harbour of le Bequet is well worth a visit. There is generous car-parking on gravelly quaysides facing an attractive mole/sea-wall, while down on the rocky foreshore a cluster of stone dwellings stand defiantly against the elements. There are good views of Cherbourg's offshore wartime forts.

Cherbourg was already developing as a trade port in the Bronze Age and was to assume a key role in the course of the Hundred Years' War. Vauban, the great seventeenth-century military architect, recognised its advantages as a harbour,

though all attempts to establish underwater foundations were thwarted by the sea for three-quarters of a century.

By the mid-1800s, however, Cherbourg's sea defences were consolidated: a 3.6km long breakwater with two piers was built by 1853, two further piers separating the large and smaller harbours (Grande and Petite Rades) following later. The city became an important naval base and arsenal, and when a Hamburg-American Line passenger ship docked in 1869, its future

scale is vastly smaller, that same raw, brassy, slightly threatening energy is here too. The persistent roar of heavy goods vehicles and the utilitarian severity of its port architecture creates an impression of industry which tends to swamp the city's attractions. Traffic is fast, few streets are pedestrianised and the overall effect can be daunting for the casual visitor.

That said, there are places of interest and sights to see. The city-centre Place Général de Gaulle in Cherbourg's old quarter is an attractive area with a variety of small shops. (The main *hypermarché* — large supermarket — is near the ferry terminals.) There is a Thursday flower market, ice-cream and pancake booths, a fruit market, cheese stalls and clothing tables extending 300m right along to Place Divette.

A new Arts complex houses, amongst much else, an art gallery containing the excellent Thomas Henry collection of paintings, many by the nineteenth-century French artist J.F. Millet. To the north near the harbour front can be found the fifteenth-century Basilique de la Trinité, a good example of the late Gothic Flamboyant style. 500m west lies the Parc Emmanuel Lias, a small enclave of tranquillity with tropical plants courtesy of the Gulf Stream's influence in this part of Normandy.

A one-time German stronghold on craggy Mont de Roule, 112m above the city, Fort du Roule is now given over to commemorating the events of World War II. Inside the Musée de la Libération, a collection of arms is kept, together with photographs, maps and uniforms, all perfectly preserved. There are exhibits of German propaganda and some artillery pieces outside. Unfortunately, the museum is vulnerable to burglary and some irreplaceable material has been lost. Even so, its commanding position and complete lack of embellishment as a

as a major transatlantic port was assured.

During World War II, heavy military equipment was landed at Cherbourg and it became the southern terminal of 'PLUTO' (Pipeline Under the Ocean), connected with the Isle of Wight and supplying the Allies with fuel. The city docks were mined and badly damaged by retreating Germans in June 1944 but were subsequently restored by the US 7th Corps.

Some have compared Cherbourg with Marseille and certainly, although the

tourist attraction imbue it with an authentic wartime atmosphere.

Cherbourg is wedded to the sea, so the wharves, arsenals and warehouses of its dockland area are its heart. There are walks alongside yacht basin quaysides, especially pleasant on fine evenings, but the industrial basins are somewhat less appealing: the naval harbour is out of bounds to foreigners. Well-sheltered by the long breakwaters between Fort de l'Ouest, Fort Central and Fort de l'Est, the Grande Rade (outer harbour) is a premier yachting location; Cherbourg is host to increasingly important Anglo-French yacht races during the summer.

Passengers with several hours to spare before or after a cross-channel trip can fill them entertainingly enough in this bustling city. It is well placed as a touring base for northern Manche, but whether or not it invites a longer stay will depend very much upon individual tastes.

At a crossroads in Querqueville village, a left turn then right leads uphill to the cemetery and parish church. On the left stands the shamrock-shaped

---

PLACES OF INTEREST IN CHERBOURG

**Place Général de Gaulle**
Shopping and market area.

**New Arts complex**
Excellent Thomas Henry collection of paintings.

**Emmanuel Lias city-centre park**
With tropical plants.

**Fort du Roule**
Liberation Museum with arms, photographs, uniforms, German propaganda.

**Dockland**
Yacht basins, wharves, cargo ships, ferries, views of great offshore breakwaters and forts.

---

sixth to eighth century Chapelle St Germain, the oldest religious building in the Cotentin, possibly in the whole of Western France. Good sea views over the Cherbourg jetties to Cap Lévy in the east and to Pointe Jardeheu in the west are gained from between church and chapel.

A little farther along the D45 coast road near Landemer, is Dur-Ecu Manor, a cluster of picturesque towers and old buildings, partly converted to an inn.

We are approaching the westernmost outpost of Normandy, a wild and rugged region where trees grow bent over in submission to prevailing winds, and a succession of rocky headlands flank secluded shingly bays. Tiny hamlets edge a landscape of field enclosures.

Well-waymarked with flashes of red and white paint, and signposted in kilometres and hours, the GR223 long-distance footpath enters its most spectacular section here. Locally named *Sentier de Littoral,* it is accessible for shorter walks from numerous points on the coast road.

Scenic narrow lanes circle out to Pointe Jardeheu and round Anse St Martin to Port Racine's toy-like harbour wall. This granite spine is Cap de la Hague. A flat tongue of land pushes bristling reefs out into the Channel; lighthouse towers, beacons and a scattering of houses stand defiantly against a bullying sea.

Offshore, the Alderney Race often runs at over eight knots — an awesome current for small craft. The only refuge hereabouts is Goury's tiny sheltered anchorage, though sheltered is hardly an adjective that springs to mind in rough weather. Two slipways radiate from the octagonal lifeboat station to facilitate launching at most states of the tide. (During the summer season it is open to visitors.)

From Auderville, near the tip of this barren promontory, Baie d'Ecalgrain unfolds, exposed and steep-sided. Extensive sands and rock-pools are uncovered at low tide, pebbles having

*Baie d'Ecalgrain*

been pushed to the beach top where storm waves gouge the earth itself. In clear conditions, the Channel Islands of Guernsey and Sark are visible, left of Alderney — separated from the mainland in fairly recent geological times.

The next headland south is reached easily by footpath but motorists follow lanes via Dannery. Nez de Jobourg is claimed as the highest cliff in Europe (a popular claim, repeated elsewhere in France!): there is no denying its impressive, windswept situation, surrounded by reefs. It is well-visited, with clifftop paths and telescopes for the wide-ranging views and sea-birds. Parking is free, if rough, and the *Auberge*

*des Grottes* tearoom/restaurant will attend to the inner man. Apart from an amusing boat-shaped kiosk on wheels selling postcards and souvenirs, the cape is refreshingly unexploited.

Dark moorland combes rise up behind the great sweep of the Anse de Vauville, as grand as any in south-west Britain. But here the illusion of nature in the raw, unblemished by the hand of man, must end.

Euphemistically called *Usine de la Hague,* a monstrous plutonium nuclear power station occupies what was once heathland and moor. Already a vast complex of futuristic towers, new roadways and enormous concrete blocks, it is festooned with cranes and

scaffolding and continues to develop, presenting a sinister face to the passer-by. Barbed wire and electric fences guard the entire site; as far away as Cherbourg protesters have stencilled 'Radioactive — Danger' and black skulls on walls and road signs. Whatever the pros and cons of the nuclear energy debate, one's sympathy goes out to local inhabitants whose remote and unspoilt promontory has been irreversibly

The landscape south and east is dotted with '-villes', small settlements off the beaten track and largely unvisited by tourists. A country church and Renaissance manor-house at Vauville nestle attractively in a hollow, while from the steep hill beyond the village of le Petit-Thot, near Camp Maneyrol gliding field, there are superlative views over the Anse de Vauville and its windswept hinterland. Another outstanding panoramic viewpoint is the Calvaire des Dunes at Biville.

Diélette, the only anchorage between Goury and Carteret, sits north of high granite cliffs, its long, graceful breakwater protecting a small harbour and low-tide sandy beach from the west. Although there is a small campsite right on the front, the resort is undeveloped

---

**PLACES OF INTEREST IN NORTH-WEST COTENTIN**

**Cap de la Hague**
Rocky cape near Alderney Race; Goury lifeboat station.

**Nez de Jobourg**
Headland cliffs above reefs; footpaths, seabirds, telescopes, small restaurant/tea-room.

**Baie d'Ecalgrain**
Large remote bay; sands, rock-pools, views of Channel Islands.

---

and used mostly by locals.

The cliff edge at Cap Flamanville stands 90m above the sea and is reached by a track from Flamanville village. There are fine clifftop walks and views span the coast south to Cap de Carteret in clear weather, when it is also possible to see the Channel Islands ranged along the horizon. Visitors may like to see Flamanville's seventeenth-century granite château, though only the surrounding parkland is open to the public.

Anse de Sciotot and Pointe du Rozel lack the wildness of the Hague promontory yet provide very pleasing coastal scenery from the little D517 corniche road. Passing through le Rozel, Surtainville and Beaubigny, Hatainville and les Moitiers can be reached.

Between here and Carteret, the D201 runs behind extensive dunes — highest on the entire Normandy seaboard.

Carteret, Barneville and Barneville-Plage effectively form a continuous settlement astride the shallow estuary of the River Gerfleur. The Gulf Stream bestows a discernible climatic advantage upon these parts of Normandy and Barneville-Carteret is a popular resort area.

Barneville's medieval church, with a fifteenth-century fortified tower, contains exquisitely decorated Romanesque arches, some capitals bearing carved animal motifs — well worth a visit. White sandy beaches stretch south for over 4km.

Carteret's quaysides, with their lobster pots, nets and impromptu seafood stalls, are backed by lively bars, shops and hotels. This is France's nearest port to Gorey on Jersey, which is visible from the nearby cape and to which there are regular sailings in summer, as well as to St Peter Port, Guernsey.

A recommended walk takes the *Sentier des Douaniers* round rocky Cap de Carteret's headland. The path is narrow in places, but not hazardously so, and leads past the lighthouse to big dunes and Carteret's second beach — Plage de la Vieille Église.

The whole resort area, while not succumbing to any excesses in tourist exploitation, is well provided with sporting and leisure amenities and lies close to unfrequented beaches and unspoilt countryside.

121

15km inland, amid wooded hills in
deepest Cotentin, stands the village of
Bricquebec, dominated by the high
polygonal tower and walls of its
fourteenth-century castle. The keep was
built on an ancient mound (*motte*) and
splendid views may be gained from the
tower's platform (160 steps). There is a
small regional museum containing
manuscripts from Mont-St-Michel and
displays of local life. A military arch,
one of the best in Manche department,
leads into a courtyard from whence the
castle looks particularly handsome.

Bricquebec also contains a Trappist
Monastery wherein Gregorian Chant
may be heard; like the castle, guided
tours are laid on for visitors. Elsewhere
in the village, a large cattle market is
held each Monday.

Apparently limitless sands and
numerous campsites reach down the
coast to the modest grey-stone harbour
frontage at Portbail. Almost lost
amongst dunes and vegetated tidal flats,
the shady village is overlooked by the
square tower of fifteenth-century Notre-
Dame-de-Portbail. Ferries leave for
Jersey from a tiny port across a
causeway over the wide and remarkably
clear-watered Ollonde estuary.

Left of the D15 inland to St Sauveur-
le-Vicomte stands the huge St Sauveur
crucifix on a wooded ridge. The village
itself was badly damaged in 1944, but its
castle ruins and a thirteenth-century
church are both worth seeing. The
church contains a fifteenth-century
statue of St James, and is on the pilgrim
route to his shrine at Santiago de
Compostela in northern Spain.

Dennerville, Surville, Bretteville-sur-
Ay and St Germain-sur-Ay — all linked
by the GR223 long-distance coastal
footpath which, of course, can be
followed for short sections — bring us to
the open estuary of the River Ay. Lessay
lies back in this inlet, its renown built
around a magnificent Benedictine
Romanesque abbey-church.
Approached along a tree-lined avenue
and flanked by pleasant grassy precincts,
it is an outstanding structure, even in a
country as rich in early monastic
churches as Normandy. Harmoniously
proportioned in mellow golden stone, it
was founded in 1056, completed by the
twelfth century, but brutally damaged in
1944. Reconstruction using the original
shattered fragments took many years:
what we witness today is a telling
monument to French tenacity. The

*Château de Bricquebec*

church's interior is austerely beautiful and the whole site well repays a visit.

Lessay's other, more fleeting attraction is a Holy Cross Fair which sees colourful tents, big horse and sheepdog sales, outdoor feasting and dancing over four days of trading and

festivities from 9 September each year.

We have reached the Cotentin Peninsula's flood-prone neck — marshland and low-lying pastures between Lessay and Carentan. Our attention now turns to the lower half of Manche department, beginning at its

*Abbaye de Lessay*

border with Calvados not far from Bayeux.

Cerisy-la-Forêt's broad main street leads north and east to many pretty walks in this delightful woodland. Not to be missed is its eleventh-century Norman Romanesque abbey church — a remarkable building of warm, pale stone, reached by a narrow lane east of the village centre.

The abbey's chequered history almost came to an end in the nineteenth century when, as the parish church of Cerisy, the demolition was ordered of the rear four bays of the nave and the monastic buildings. The stone thus released was sold for house-building and road-paving. Serious restoration of this notable building only began some fifty years ago on the initiative of the newly-formed 'Friends of the Abbey', and such has been the scale of the work involved that it continues today: explanatory photographs are displayed inside.

In July 1944, 4,200 tons of bombs fell on the strategic road and rail junction of St Lô in the space of just ninety minutes: the town, virtually obliterated, was dubbed at the time 'Capital of the Ruins'. Twenty years were to pass before rebuilding was complete and, sad to say, its unremarkable slabby, post-war architecture seems to indicate an opportunity lost for more adventurous and aesthetically-pleasing solutions.

Serving only to point up how much has gone, the dramatic outlines of the old quarter — the medieval *Enclos* — are still preserved in the upper town, while restoration of the wrecked fourteenth to fifteenth century Notre-Dame continues to this day. Damaged towers on its west front are graphic reminders of the holocaust half a century ago.

All is not gloom in St Lô, however — far from it! The town's situation on a rocky spur above the River Vire is revealed by its new configuration and the place is busy and prosperous, a good touring centre for Manche.

A Musée des Beaux-Arts in the Hôtel-de-Ville houses an excellent art collection, including valuable sixteenth-century tapestries, and there is a large mosaic by the artist Ferdnand Léger on a façade of the jointly-built French-American Memorial Hospital, south-west of the town centre.

Near St Lô's eastern perimeter may be found the famous Stud (*Haras*) with its full complement of 150 thoroughbred Norman and English stallions present from mid-July to mid-February.

Torigni-sur-Vire's handsome sixteenth-century Matignon château is another post-war reconstruction, but faithfully carried out and subsequently restored. Its east wing contains Louis XIII and Louis XIV furniture and tapestries. (One of the Matignon family married a Grimaldi and became a Prince of Monaco.) Shady parkland in which the building is set offers the visitor boating lakes, wooded walks and ample opportunities for picnics.

West of Torigni, off the D551, an abrupt edge of rock hangs above the River Vire where it has carved a big semicircular slice from vegetated shale cliffs on its sinuous course through a pastoral landscape. Not quite as dramatic as Roche d'Oëtre in Suisse

PLACES OF INTEREST IN AND AROUND ST LÔ

**St Lô**
Excellent art collection in the Hôtel-de-Ville. Also, over 150 thoroughbred Norman and English stallions to be seen at the famous stud.

**Cerisy-la-Forêt, 18km north-east**
Marvellous eleventh-century Romanesque abbey-church. Woodland walks.

**Château de Matignon, Torigni-sur-Vire**
Furniture and tapestries, boating lake, walks. Nearby Roches de Ham cliff-edge viewpoint over Vire valley.

**Coutances**
Imposing Norman Gothic cathedral of great interest. Good shops and restaurants. Outstanding public gardens.

Normande, the Roches de Ham nonetheless form an entertaining vantage point. Views from the first platform soar 80m to the river below, whose valley is further revealed from the second platform. Parking is free in an adjacent field.

No distance away to the south on an attractive terrace of land overlooking the Vire and Jacre valleys is a 62-acre park of beech, lime and cedar. At its centre, Château de l'Angotière is open to the public; a smart and historic building, though not outstanding. Within are a good collection of old ceramics from the China and India Companies and eighteenth-century furniture. As the château is occupied, visits are in guided tours. (Please note: it is closed July, Easter and weekends. A fee is payable even to drive through the grounds!)

Typical *bocage* countryside hereabouts loosens its grip as progress is

*Abbaye de Hambye*

made westwards. From the Mont Robin
Calvary, 1.5km across a field from the
D999, views open out to Suisse
Normande in the east, Coutances
cathedral in the north-west and even the
Channel Islands if the air is very clear.

Like so many ancient buildings in
Normandy, the fabric of Abbaye de
Hambye has weathered to blend into its
natural hollow by the River Sienne.
These Romanesque ruins are immensely
evocative — a great soaring shell of
walls, arches and columns, some bearing
centuries of names carved into their soft
stone. Birds fly through sightless

windows and grass now carpets the choir
and nave, yet although the abbey lacks
its former glory, the site still possesses
qualities to inspire. Best viewpoints are
from the narrow B258 to Percy and from
the entrance archway.

The conventual buildings are restored
and include a typical Norman Gothic
chapter house. Inside are found a small
frescoed 'Hall of the Dead', a library
with excavated lapidary objects, a
kitchen with a truly monumental
chimneypiece and a fourteenth-century
wooden statue of Christ. The lay-
brothers' former refectory is hung with

*Centuries of inscribed names, Abbaye de Hambye*

seventeenth-century Rouen tapestries
and has period furnishings.

Concerts and conferences are held in
the upstairs dormitory and the site is
open most days all year except January.
English-language scripts to accompany a
visit are available from the entrance
room (turn left up steps).

Coutances, religious centre of the
Cotentin, stands on a hill 10km from the
coast, its exceptionally striking Norman
Gothic Cathédrale Notre-Dame a

conspicuous feature from far and wide. Seen from Place du Parvis, it is one of Normandy's most impressive ecclesiastical buildings, a marvel of Norman Gothic construction in light stone, its proportions vast yet its detail surprisingly delicate.

Begun in 1218, the cathedral incorporated parts of a former Romanesque structure. The west front has two towers over 77m high, and one should stand at the centre of the transept to admire the domed elegance of the fabulous octagonal lantern-tower, rising above to 41m at its apex. Also to be seen are some superb stained glass windows from the thirteenth century, and a fourteenth-century statue of Notre-Dame-de-Coutances in the central chapel of the apse.

Coutances, in common with so much of this region, received heavy damage in World War II. Today, however, the scars are healed and there are excellent shops and restaurants. Monday is market day.

The Jardin Public is outstanding. Terraced and laid out in seventeenth-century style, its various levels have been provided with statues, benches and small ponds. Flower beds are lavish and unusual in design; some have clocks, cars and railway engines incorporated as motifs and there are many rare and beautiful trees. At the gardens' entrance, the former Hôtel Poupinel houses a local museum with pottery, paintings and *objets d'art*. Views from these gardens can be extensive. Look particularly for three arches of the thirteenth-century aqueduct, built on the site of an earlier Roman one: they lie just to the north-west in the verdant Bulsard valley.

To the right of the D244 at Gratot, 5km north-west of Coutances, stands an extraordinary cluster of four crumbling towers around the courtyard of Manoir d'Argouges. Moat and ramparts date back to the fourteenth century, though some additions were made as late as the eighteenth century. The original manor, as depicted in paintings of the time, was even more extravagant than today's curiosity. A pleasant, rather agricultural approach behind a church leads across the wide moat to the main archway entrance.

An imposing white statue in the village of Tourville-sur-Sienne, 6km east, is of Admiral de Tourville who lost the Battle of Cap de la Hague. There are wide views just down the road from the statue in the village cemetery.

Back on the coast, country to the south of Lessay is windswept and harshly beautiful — a level wasteland of gorse and scrub mildly reminiscent of the Camargue. Unlikely though it may seem, the light sandy soil of the 'Lande de Lessay' (*lande* means heath or sandy moor) is intensively cultivated on the landward side. Motorists and cyclists on the D650 coast road will pass long fields of onions and carrots, some under cloches, parcelled off by hedgerows. Myriad minor roads and tracks connect with remote beaches one or two kilometres away and campsites are in good supply.

All along the sea's open and breezy edge, beaches are enormous, especially at low tide. Holiday development being low-key — mostly tents, caravans and chalets — there is always plenty of scope to 'get away from it all' in the dunes. Sea-bathing, however, is not always safe or life-guarded, and the big tides should be watched carefully for the threat they pose to the unwary, particularly where there are sandbanks.

Coutainville is perhaps Manche's most up-to-date and forward looking resort. It is flanked by 7km of those same vast sandy beaches and the benificent Gulf Stream allows sub-tropical vegetation to clothe the hilly hinterland behind the dunes. Pretty encircling countryside holds secluded old manor-houses in charming sheltered valleys.

Coutainville, in collaboration with neighbouring Agon, has directed the thrust of its development towards providing modern holiday amenities:

*Part of Château de Crèvecoeur-en-Auge*

*Cabourg*

*British War Cemetery, Douvres-la-Délivrande*

*Château de Fontaine-Henry*

there is a casino, theatre, racecourse, golf course, swimming pools, facilities for water-skiing and scuba-diving, tennis, horse-riding, cycles for hire and angling. Old-fashioned beach huts have been superseded by shady 'South Sea Island' straw huts.

At low spring tides, locals flock to the exposed mud and flat rock beds near the water's edge. Equipped with shovels, baskets, waterproofs and waders, they are out to harvest shellfish and lugworms. All human scale seems lost as hundreds of tiny figures dot the shallows and sandbanks.

Past the broad marshy outlet of the River Vanlee, crossed by a causeway at low tide, Granville's old town rises ahead on a granite promontory — Pointe du Roc, the northern limit of the Baie du Mont-St-Michel. The lower town, on land partly reclaimed from the sea, is a bustling, animated place during the summer and other public holidays. On a little-known secondary rail link from Paris, the resort attracts large numbers in the season — a fact reflected in a constellation of shops, cafés, bars and restaurants lining its narrow streets.

Granville's port is protected by scalloped concrete harbour walls and its sizeable fishing fleet provides a plethora of fascinating sights and smells along the quaysides. In addition to handling commercial cargo, the port provides generous mooring for pleasure craft and is something of a yachting centre for these waters. Large crowds congregate in early August for a Breton-like 'Pardon of the Sea'.

Ferries run to Jersey and to the rugged Iles Chausey, a popular day-trip. This small archipelago of granite islands, rocks and reefs is uninhabited except for a few fishermen and their families on la Grande Ile, the only point of access for visitors. Privately owned, the islands were once quarried for brown granite used, amongst many other places, in the building of Mont-St-Michel. It is easy to walk around Grande Ile (it is only 2km long) for a sight of its

forts, lighthouse, church and offshore rocks.

Granville's citadel was constructed by the English in 1439 to consolidate their position against the threat from French-held Mont-St-Michel, but it fell nevertheless two years later. A circuit may be made of the ramparts enclosing the somewhat severe Haute Ville (granite is a hard building material to work). Its warren of narrow streets and arches is dominated at the western end by the massive fifteenth-seventeenth century Notre-Dame church, while the Musée du Vieux Granville is located in the Grande Porte.

In stormy weather, spectacular views are gained from Rue du Nord, while in clear conditions distant Brittany can be glimpsed from the large Place de l'Isthme.

Granville's military barracks, a cheerless hulk out on Pointe du Roc, is juxtaposed with relics of German World War II fortifications: a lone gun barrel on concrete plinths still stands sentinel over the northern approaches. From near the red-topped lighthouse, a path circumvents the little rocky point itself — an awe-inspiring walk in rough weather.

Granville, perhaps a little indulgently, has been dubbed 'Monaco of the North' after its casino and headland rock. Busy and varied it is, however, and a centre for thalassotherapy (sea-water cures). There are pleasant walks in the Jardin Public Christian-Dior (of coutourier fame), giving access along a cliff path to the immense beach at Donville-les-Bains. Granville's own is altogether narrower beneath shaly cliffs, but does enjoy the bonus of a swimming pool.

By taking the D924 east for some twenty kilometres, visitors will arrive at Champrepus and its Parc Zoologique. Eighty different species of birds and animals are represented, from apes to bears, tigers to deer, peacocks to kangaroos, and there are all the ancillary services to make a family outing here enjoyable, including a souvenir shop.

Creatures roam in semi-freedom and the zoo-park is open from March to the end of December.

Once in this vicinity, do not miss the cheerful brass and copper town of Villedieu-les-Poëles. *Poëles* are pots or frying pans, and for over 800 years Villedieu has specialised in making copperware, notably the great round-bellied milk flagons (*cannes*) once found on every Norman farm.

Today, craftsmen make a wide range of kitchen utensils in copper, brass and aluminium as well as souvenirs in glass and pewter. The *poëles* shops seem very lugubrious, immaculate displays of highly polished ware meticulously arranged for the passing tourists. One wonders how so many shops retailing essentially the same products can survive, let along prosper. Perhaps subtle variations in emphasis provide shoppers with the choice needed to make a truly individual purchase.

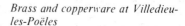

several pleasant sites in the town.

Before exploring the final corner of Manche around the Baie du Mont-St-Michel, an excursion will be made inland to visit the picturesque town of Mortain in the upper valley of the River Sée.

Situated on the flanks of a rocky hillside in undulating, wooded country at the edge of Parc Régional Normandie-Maine, Mortain is a popular and busy tourist centre. Apart from its surviving antiquities, the town is post-war, having been virtually destroyed by a violent German counterattack towards the end of the war in August 1944.

Église St Evroult is all-dominating, a thirteenth-century Gothic limestone edifice. 1km north stands the twelfth-century former Cistercian Abbaye Blanche. Unexpectedly, its stone is dark, *blanche* referring to the undyed habits its monks once wore. In any case, what remains is mostly a nineteenth-century addition, though the well-proportioned cloister is Romanesque.

Below the abbey, the River Cance jumps and spumes in a wooded gorge

Villedieu's bell-foundry (*Fonderie des Cloches*) is one of only a few of its kind left in the whole world. Bells are seen cast by methods unchanged down the centuries and the foundry, in Rue du Pont Chignon, should not be missed.

Also worth finding are a Museum of Copperware and Stove-making, and a Furniture Museum with 130 pieces from Rouen and Vire on display. Thirteenth-century Notre-Dame de l'Ospital, built by the Knights of St John, is one of

---

**PLACES OF INTEREST IN AND AROUND VILLEDIEU-LES-POËLES**

**Villedieu**
Brass and copper centre; utensils and souvenirs in shops; rare bell foundry; Museum of Copperware and Stove-making.

**Champrepus zoo-park, 7km to the west**
80 species of animals and birds in semi-freedom; refreshments, souvenirs.

**Abbaye de Hambye, 15 km north by River Sienne**
Evocative abbey ruins, and restored conventual buildings with period interiors.

*The 'Grande Cascade', Mortain*

and is reached by paths from Avenue de l'Abbaye Blanche and from the bridge on a lane branching down left of the town centre. Red and white paint waymarks indicate that the lane is on the long-distance GR22 footpath from Paris to Mont-St-Michel. River shallows are crossed on little plank bridges and viewpoints abound amongst the boulders and trees. Highlight of this most picturesque forest-glade setting is the 'Grande Cascade', a delightful waterfall tumbling 25m down rocky steps. Once painted by Courbet, the scene is replete with mystery and atmosphere.

A further waterfall — 'Petite Cascade' — is actually higher, with a drop of some 35m. To reach it, go downhill from Place du Château, cross the Cance and take a narrow path past the Aiguille rock. A tributary stream is crossed on stepping stones and followed to a rock amphitheatre over which the waterfall flows.

From Granville to Mont-St-Michel, the coastline is drawn in by the mouth of the River Sélune. Beaches of shaly sand run south through little-visited St Pair to Jullouville and the smart pine-shaded bars and villas at Carolles-Plage, with its marvellous family beach.

The attractiveness of the coast itself diminishes towards Genêts, and bathing becomes more hazardous. Tides here are immense — an impetuous sea rising and sinking between horizon and foreshore. Clifftops that concealed Mont-St-Michel from view farther north are no longer a hindrance and in clear weather the magical pyramid floats enticingly above tidal flats.

Each July a pilgrimage is made right across the sands to the great abbey-church, but at other times, individuals are warned against attempting this eight to nine kilometre walk without the services of an experienced guide (apply to the Place des Halles, Genêts).

Perched 100m above the Sée estuary, Avranches is a town best explored on foot, when its maze of alleyways, nooks and crannies and its unsurpassed views to Mont-St-Michel can be appreciated at leisure. For lovers of old buildings it is a delight: be sure to see Rue Engibault, Place Littre and St Gervais church.

Avranches' cathedral was destroyed in 1794 during the French Revolution — all that is left are a few excavated remains. An eighth-century bishop of this charming old town founded Mont-St-Michel, so, predictably, there are significant historical connections. Musée d'Avranchin contains important manuscripts, dating from the eighth to fifteenth centuries, in this context.

A paving slab (the *Plate-forme*) in the gardens of the Sous-Prefecture in Place Daniel-Huet commemorates the spot where Henry II of England knelt in penance for the murder of Thomas-à-Becket.

Imposition of a Salt Tax in western France during 1639 resulted in a revolt by Avranchin saltworkers. Armed bands, led by Jean Quétil ('John Barefoot') rampaged through local towns and countryside in protest, though this manifestation of the fiercely independent Norman spirit was subsequently repressed.

Best sea views are from the edge of the colourful Jardin des Plantes, whence distant Mont-St-Michel and adjacent Tombelaine may be viewed by telescope. For a closer and altogether more dramatic inspection of the islands, flights round the bay operate from an airfield south-west of the town, except at very high tides when it is prone to inundation.

The coast road from Pontaubault is all apple orchards and large reclaimed fields of palest clay soil. Even for first-time visitors, Mont-St-Michel is likely to seem oddly familiar. For most of us it has become a cliché as common as the Matterhorn or the Eiffel Tower and, outside Paris, is France's — even Europe's — most popular tourist destination.

Though the volume of present-day sightseers is quite staggering, the site has been busy with pilgrims for many centuries. During the Middle Ages — when it was not connected to the mainland and known as 'Mont-St-Michel au péril de la mer' — there was drinking at the inns, sometimes a night's free lodging in the Aumônerie, then souvenir flasks filled with sand to be bought, taken home and proudly shown round.

But what of its origins? It is thought that a series of tidal surges during the eighth century permanently drowned the forest surrounding two granite outcrops in the Couesnon estuary. Huge deposits of mud and quicksand so altered the

pattern of tidal flow that the rocks
became established island features.
Tombelaine, 4km out in the bay,
remains so today, but the island nearest
the shoreline, known as Mont Tombe,
was accessible at low tide and a tiny
chapel was erected on its summit in AD
709.

Three centuries passed before the
great abbey was begun, another three
before its well-nigh impregnable
fortifications were added, rendering it
inviolate despite years of sporadic
harassment by the English. Only during
the Middle Ages did any form of
commercial exploitation develop, with

The 1.8km causeway was constructed in 1879, bringing to an end the periodic drowning of luckless visitors caught out by the fierce tides. It is impossible not to be moved by the cascading architecture of this small terraced city with its ancient dwellings on steep streets, its flights of steps above dizzy verticalities, its engirdling walls and bastions, all crowned by the gilded statue of St Michel atop the abbey-church spire.

To do justice to Mont-St-Michel, allow at least half a day, preferably outside July and August. If practicable, a late arrival and overnight stay in one of the small hotels allows a tour of the ramparts and Abbey to be made before the day-trip coaches arrive. (Accommodation list, but not reservations, from the *Syndicat d'Initiative*).

From the large causeway car park (under water at times posted at the entrance!) access to the Mount is via Porte du Roi, leading into the only street — Grande Rue. Shops sell vulgar ceramics, jewellery, snowstorm paperweights and endless knick-knacks to satisfy an appetite for souvenirs: in common with many tourist meccas, there is the narrowest of choices between gimmicky kitsch items! Judging by the postcards for sale, Mont-St-Michel is probably the most photographed place in Europe — there are shots from every conceivable angle and in all lights and seasons.

Grande Rue climbs steeply towards the Abbey summit. Cosy little bars, cafés and restaurants beckon and a commissionaire outside the Musée Historial vocally musters passers-by. (There is another Musée Historique at the foot of the Abbey). Steps lead on up past huddles of granite houses to the ramparts walk and good sea views. Tombelaine is just over 2km north. Once occupied by the English in the seventeenth century — remains of a fort

craftsmen and innkeepers prospering. The French Revolution saw the monks dispersed and the buildings looted; in the late 1700s Napoleon turned the Mount into a prison. These sad years of decadence and decline prevailed until a century ago when the State assumed responsibility and began restoration.

*Porte du Roi, Mont-St-Michel*

still exist — it must have been a miserable posting indeed!

A guided tour of the Abbey lasts about an hour and, it must be said, is not cheap. (But it is half-price on Sundays and Feast Days; there are reduced rates for parties.) However, the internal splendours are hardly less spectacular than those outside and do fill out the visitor's appreciation of the Mount's history. English commentary is available in August.

Conducted tours begin in the Aumônerie, proceeding through magnificent rooms to the second floor Cloister with its 227 graceful columns. This is the thirteenth-century 'Merveille', an impressive component of the abbey complex. Many architectural styles from the tenth to the sixteenth century are embodied in the Abbey itself, which rises to 182m above sea level. Sensational panoramas over the island, sea and mainland are obtained from an external gallery.

For a small fee, the Abbey gardens may be visited, providing good views from below of the soaring 'Merveille' and of the Baie du Mont-St-Michel. For detailed information on all aspects of the

## THE MAIN SIGHTS OF MONT-ST-MICHEL

**Grande Rue**
Shopping street: food stalls, souvenirs galore, bars, cafés, restaurants.

**Two History museums**
Many half-timbered medieval granite houses.

**Guided tours**
Of the great Abbey complex.

**Wide-ranging views**
Over the bay from ramparts walk.

**Abbey gardens**

**A walk round the Mount's base**
At low tide; 8km guided walk across the entire bay's sandbanks from Genêts.

Mount, consult the *Syndicat d'Initiative* in the old Guard Room, left of the Porte du Roi entrance. (Open through the summer.)

While at such times as the Festival of Archangel Michael in late September, and throughout much of the low season, Mont-St-Michel is at its best, it can be a disappointment in high summer when the crush of fellow visitors swamps any real sense of history. Systems of organising and directing human traffic resemble a conveyor-belt, but in summer need to be slick just to cope with the numbers involved. In his time, Ruskin was appalled by the squalor and filth he found associated with the crowds: today, at least, we are spared that particular unpleasantness!

Barefoot or in wellington boots, it is possible to walk right round the almost circular base of the Mount. Be armed, however, with knowledge of the tides,

for here they are phenomenal, surging in at a metre a second across 14km of sandbanks and mud flats. Depending upon the moon's phase and weather conditions, Mont-St-Michel is only a true island at the highest equinoctial tides and even then the causeway stays dry. But differences between high and low water are greater in this bay than anywhere else in continental Europe, and may exceed 18m.

Pontorson, a short distance inland, is largely a service town for Mont-St-Michel, providing accommodation and eating places for many of the 750,000 or so sightseers per year who arrive here. The River Couesnon marks Normandy's border with Brittany, and from its banks Mont-St-Michel is once again a remote, ethereal pyramid — perhaps at its most evocative seen thus across tidal shallows and saltings.

# Further Information

State-run museums, art galleries and public monuments are usually open from 9 or 10am till noon, and 2pm to 7pm during the summer season, with shorter hours in winter. Tuesday is a common closing day, as are French public holidays: 1 Jan (New Year's Day), Easter Sunday and Monday, 1 May (Labour Day), 8 May (VE Day), Ascension Day, Whit Sunday and Monday, 14 July (Bastille Day), 15 August (Assumption Day), 1 November (All Saints Day), 11 November (Remembrance Day) and Christmas Day.

Visitors to public monuments, notable buildings and some museums are often shown round in guided groups rather than allowed individual access. Even if French is not understood, this system is unlikely to detract from your enjoyment. An entry fee is usually charged. Opening times are only shown in the following list if they differ significantly from those above.

Many country churches and chapels are opened on demand and a local enquiry will normally yield the key's custodian. Such buildings are too numerous for inclusion in this guide.

Every sizeable town and resort — many of the smaller ones too — has a tourist information centre called an *Office de Tourism, Maison de Tourism* or *Syndicat d'Initiative*. Visitors can obtain details of local accommodation and campsites, excursions, beauty spots and special events. Information of a more general nature, including travel to and within France, will be provided on request by the French Government Tourist Office, 178 Piccadilly, London W1V 0AL; or the French Government Tourist Office, 610 5th Avenue, New York, New York.

Museums, art galleries, historic and ecclesiastical buildings open to the public, wildlife and amusement parks, and other places of interest.

## CHAPTER 1 — SEINE-MARITIME

### Clères
Musée des Automobiles de Normandie
Open: daily 8am-8pm.
Cars, military vehicles, vintage cycles, aircraft.

Parc Ornithologique
Open: 1 April to 30 September, daily.
Many exotic birds, some wild animals.

### Dieppe
Musée du Château
Open: 15 June to 15 September.
Impressionist paintings, model ships, seventeenth-century carved ivories, and much else.

Musée de la Guerre et du Raid, near Pourville-sur-Mer
Open: Easter to 30 September, closed Monday.
Tanks, guns etc of World War II and Dieppe Raid of August 1942.

### Étretat
Musée Nungesser et Coli
Open: weekends only, Easter and June to September.

Museum to pioneer French aviators.

### Eu
Château d'Eu
Open: 1 April to 31 October.
Huge château in parkland, beautiful Louis Philippe interior.

## Fécamp
Musée de la Bénédictine
Open: Easter to 11 November.
Medieval and Renaissance art objects,
history of famous liqueur, visit to
modern distillery and tasting.

## Forges-les-Eaux
Musée des faïences
Open: Tuesday to Friday.
Collection of *faïence* pottery in town
hall.

## Le Havre
Musée des Beaux-Arts (André Malraux).
Modern galleries housing important
collection of paintings, tapestries, glass,
etc.

Musée de Vieux Havre
Closed Monday and Tuesday.
Pottery, documents, models, engravings
in restored seventeenth-century house.

## Jumièges
Abbaye de Jumièges
Closed Tuesday and Wednesday in
winter.
One of France's great ruins.

## Lillebonne
Remains of second-century Roman
amphitheatre, and a museum of Gallo-
Roman artefacts in Town Hall; apply to
Café de l'Hôtel-de-Ville to visit.

## Manoir d'Ango
Open: daily.
Splendid manor-house with huge central
dovecote and half-timbered
outbuildings.

## Neufchâtel-en-Bray
Musée Mathon-Durand
Open: weekends.
Pays de Bray arts and crafts, well, cider-
mill and press.

## Rouen
Musée de Jeanne d'Arc
Open: daily in summer, closed winter
Monday.

Waxwork scenes, collection of books
and documents.

Musée des Beaux-Arts.
Normandy's finest art gallery. Rouen
ceramics, large collection of paintings by
Dutch, Italian, Flemish, Spanish schools
and French Impressionists. Many
famous works. Entry fee covers Gros-
Horloge and Musée de Ferronnerie.

Musée de Ferronnerie
Closed Tuesday and Wednesday mornings.
Unusual exhibition of decorative
ironwork; over 14,000 items.

Gros-Horloge
Open: Easter to 1 October.
Inner workings of medieval clock, views
of city.

Musée Corneille
Closed Thursday, Friday mornings and
holidays.
Birthplace and house of Pierre Corneille
— furniture, original books.

Musée de Flaubert et l'Histoire de la
Médecine
Closed Sunday and Monday.
Books, furniture and effects, Flaubert
family's surgical equipment.

Musée des Antiquités
Closed Thursday.
In seventeenth-century cloister —
paintings, religious treasure, tapestries,
icons, Gallo-Roman material, prehistory
and Natural History.

Musée d'Art Populaire Normand, 16km
east at Martainville
Closed Tuesday and Wednesday.
Splendid fifteenth-century château with
museum of Norman rural life from
Middle Ages to eighteenth century.

## Villequier
Musée de Victor Hugo
Closed winter Monday and Tuesday.
Dedicated to the writer, his family, with
letters, furniture, portraits and
ornaments.

## Abbaye de St Wandrille
Open: Sunday and holidays; guided

groups only on Monday-Friday late afternoons.

Tithe-barn church, splendid ruins, Gregorian Chant.

---

## CHAPTER 2 — EURE

### Beaumesnil Château
Park open Monday to Saturday, closed August.
Magnificent Louis XIII château and formal gardens.

### Le Bec-Hellouin
Abbaye du Bec-Hellouin
Open: daily.
Noble ruins of historic abbey, small museum and pottery.

Musée des Vieilles Voitures
Open: daily.
Fifty vintage cars in working order.

### Bernay
Musée Municipal de Bernay.
*Faïence* pottery from Rouen, Delft and Nevers; French and Dutch paintings, local history.

### Champ-de-Bataille Château
Open: 15 March to 30 June, Sunday and Monday; 1 July to 14 September, Thursday - Monday; 15 September to 14 March, Sunday.
Stately château in deer forest — paintings, sculptures, tapestries, rare *objets d'art,* period furnishings, events in grounds.

### Evreux
Musée Municipal d'Evreux
Open: Tuesday to Saturday and Sunday afternoon.
Local prehistoric finds, Gallo-Roman exhibits, sixteenth to eightenth-century paintings, *objets d'art* and furniture, all in former archbishop's palace.

### Fontaine-Guérard Abbaye
Open: 1 March to 30 September.

Extensive abbey ruins by River Andelle; Chapter House, monks' dormitory and workroom.

### Gaillard Château
Open: 15 March to 15 October, closed Tuesday and Wednesday morning.
Spectacular castle ruins on rocky spur above Seine. Entry fee also admits to:

Musée de Nicolas Poussin
Closed Tuesday and February.
Poussin's art and local exhibits. Located in les Andelys.

### Gisors
Château de Gisors
Closed 15 December to 31 January.
Twelve towers linked by curtain walls, great circular keep, Prisoners' Tower with oven, well and chimney; prisoners' grafitti in dungeon dating from fourteenth century.

### Giverny
Musée Claude Monet
Open: April to October, closed Monday.
Monet's house, studio and water garden, carefully preserved.

### Harcourt Château
Closed winter weekends and 16 November to end February.
Impressive feudal castle, period interior, moat walk, exhibitions, large arboretum.

### Louviers
Musée Municipal de Louviers.
Local costume, lace, furniture and paintings.

### Mortemer Abbaye
Open: 1 April to 15 November.
One of France's most evocative relics of Medieval Christendom, many historic associations; set deep in Forêt de Lyons.

### Pont-Audemer
Musée Canal
Closed Sunday.
Curious collections, including over 10,000 insects.

Musée Memorial de la Résistance et de la Déportation
Visits on application.
Town Hall display of local 1940-44 Resistance documents.

**Seine River**
Details of summer cruises from Normandy Tourism, 78, Rue Jeanne d'Arc, 76000 ROUEN; and Novel Tour, 15, Rue de Crosne, 76000 ROUEN.

**Vernon**
Château Bizy
Open: 1 April to 1 November, closed Tuesday and some Saturdays.
Classical eighteenth-century country house, mementoes of Napoleon and his marshals.

Musée Poulain
New museum with varied paintings, sculpture, local history and touring exhibitions.

# CHAPTER 3 — ORNE

**L'Aigle**
Musée Juin 1944
Closed winter Mondays.
Uniformed wax figures, recorded voices of Allied leaders, atmosphere of later stages of Battle of Normandy. Next to Town Hall.

**Alençon**
École Dentellière (Lace Museum)
Closed Sunday and Monday mornings.
Old-established state-run lacemaking school. See lace being made, items for sale.

Musée de Peinture
Closed Mondays and May Day. In Town Hall.
Alençon lace and French paintings.

**Argentan**
Le Point d'Argentan
Closed weekends.
Lace workshop and stitch-lace museum run by nuns at Benedictine Abbey.

Haras du Pin (National Stud).
Full complement of stallions present 15 July to 15 February. Apply to Lodge for free, groom-accompanied tour. Located 15km east of Argentan.

**Carrouges Château**
Closed Tuesday.
Magnificent brick and stone château in formal gardens; opulent interior, portrait gallery.

**La Ferté-Macé**
Musée de la Ferté-Macé
Open: Thursday only.
Devoted to local artist, Léandhe de la Touche.

**Flers**
Musée de Flers
Open: Easter to 15 October.
Seventeenth-nineteenth-century paintings, material on cotton-weaving, farming and local life.

**O Château**
Open: daily.
Best known of Orne châteaux — ornate, wide moat, walks in grounds. Adjacent Ferme d'O.

**Sées**
Cathédrale St Latrium
Interior closed Wednesdays.

Musée d'Art Religieux
Open: Easter to 30 September.
French religious art through the centuries.

# CHAPTER 4 — CALVADOS

**Arromanches**
Musée du Débarquement
Closed Christmas Day.
Principal Landings Museum — film, weapons, uniforms, photographs, plans and maps, autographs, dioramas, artillery. Remains of Mulberry Harbour visible offshore.

**Balleroy**
Château de Balleroy
Closed Wednesday and mid-June week.
Landscaped gardens, classical façade,
rich interior.

Musée des Ballons
Opening times as for château.
Unique exhibition of ballooning, from
Montgolfier to present.

**Bayeux**
Centre de Guillaume-le-Conquérant.
The Bayeux Tapestry, closed Christmas
and New Year's Day.
Audio-visual displays, film, explanatory
material, the Tapestry itself, with
English commentary.

Musée Baron-Gérard
Opening times as for Tapestry.
Impressionist paintings, porcelain,
Bayeux lace, Rouen ceramics, local
paintings, Flemish and Italian sixteenth-
century primitives.

Musée de la Bataille de Normandie
Open: daily; 1 November to 31 March,
weekends only.
Devoted to events of June/July 1944.

Cathédrale Notre-Dame
Floodlit July to mid-September.

**Brécy Château**
Open: afternoons, closed Wednesday.
Large seventeenth-century gateway,
topiary, terraced gardens, views, fine
chimneypieces.

**Caen**
Musée des Beaux-Arts
Closed Tuesday and public holidays.
Modern galleries in Caen castle —
Venetian, Flemish, French paintings
from sixteenth to early twentieth
century; enamels, porcelain, miniatures,
gold and silver, tapestries, furniture,
engravings from large collection.

Musée de Normandie
Opening times as for art gallery.
Normandy folklore, farm life, costume,
local crafts.

Chapelle de St Georges
Opening times as for castle.
Twelfth-century chapel remembering
those who died in Battle for Caen, 1944.

**Cerisy-la-Forêt**
Abbey Conventual Buildings
Open: 15 March to 11 November,
Sunday and holidays; 1 July to 15
September, daily (except Sunday).
Lapidary museum, Abbot's Chapel,
documents, furniture.

**Clécy**
Musée des Antiquités Normandes
Open: 1 July to 15 September,
afternoons; Easter to 30 June and 16
September to 31 October, Sundays and
holidays only; closed 1 November to
Easter.
Antiques, local crafts, folklore, cider-
tasting, miniature railway in leisure
park. Impressive château.

**Falaise**
Château de Falaise
Closed Tuesday, October and Sundays in
winter.
Keep, massive round tower and walls,
dungeon, Great Hall, birthplace of
William the Conqueror.

La Ferme de St Quentin, 9.5km north
Open: Easter to 30 September,
afternoons; October, weekend
afternoons; closed November to Easter.
Small museum of regional agriculture on
farm.

**Fontaine-Henry Château**
Open: Easter to 31 May and 1
September to mid-October, afternoons;
winter, Sundays and holidays only.
Fascinating château architecture, fine
interior with antiques, paintings and
sculptures.

**Honfleur**
Musée d'Art Populaire Normande
Closed Friday.
Local history in displays and interiors.

Musée de la Marine
Open: 1 July to 15 September, Saturday -
Thursday, and winter weekends.
Life and work of local fishermen.
Located by Vieux Bassin.

Musée Eugène-Boudin
Open: daily, afternoons only on winter
weekdays.
Works by Boudin and many well known
artists besides; Norman costume,
modern exhibitions.

## Lisieux
Ste Thérèse Basilica
Open: Easter to 15 October.
Vast Romano-Byzantine structure,
processional way, views from dome,
floodlit summer evenings, material on
Ste Thérèse's life in crypt

Diorama de Ste Thérèse
Open: 1 March to 15 December.
Wax models and displays

Ste Thérèse's life as a Carmelite - display
in North Cloister
Open: 15 March to 31 October.

Musée du Vieux Lisieux
Closed 15 December to 30 January.
Pays d'Auge pottery, costumes, Roman
coins.

## Lisores
Musée Ferdnand Léger
Open: daily.
Artist's life and work displayed in
converted barn.

## Ouistreham Riva-Bella
Musée du Débarquement
Closed 15 September to Palm Sunday.
Weapons and equipment of World War
II in small museum.

## Pontécoulant Château
Closed Tuesday and October.
Fine sixteenth to eighteenth-century
château in parkland, furniture museum;
trips in nearby Suisse Normande.

## St Gabriel Château
Closed Wednesday.

Magnificent classical doorway, beautiful
gardens.

## Trouville
Musée Montebello
Open: 16 June to 15 September,
afternoons; Easter to 15 June, weekend
afternoons only.
Paintings by Boudin, Jongkind and
others.

---

# CHAPTER 5 — MANCHE

## Avranches
Musée d'Avranchin
Open: Easter to 30 September.
Eighth to fifteenth century manuscripts
from Mont-St-Michel; temporary
regional exhibitions.

Jardin des Plantes
Open: all year.
Waterfall, rare trees, coastal views,
illuminations and commentary.

Flights round Mont-St-Michel from
airfield to south; take D456 and D556.

## Barfleur
Gatteville lighthouse
Open: daily, apply to keeper.

## Bricquebec
Château de Bricquebec.
Open: July and August.
Fine fourteenth-century castle,
polygonal tower, good military arch.

Musée d'Archéologie et Ethnographie
Régional, located in castle tower
Open: July and August.
Manuscripts from Mont-St-Michel,
displays of regional life, minerals;
thirteenth-century restored crypt in
south buildings.

## Cherbourg
Musée Thomas Henry, in new Arts
complex
Open: daily.
Furniture displays and paintings,
especially good collection by J.F. Millet.

Musée de la Libération
Closed Tuesday.
Weapons, photographs, maps and
uniforms, German propoganda in
hilltop Fort du Roule.

## Coutances
Manoir d'Argouges, 4km west
Open: 1 July to 1 September; other times
Sunday only.
Eccentric, towered manor-house from
fourteenth century.

Jardin Public
Open: daily.

## Granville
Excursions to Iles Chausey and Jersey.

Aquarium
Open: Palm Sunday to 1 November.
Local species, tropical fish and sealions.
Located on Pointe du Roc.

Musée du Vieux Granville
Open: Easter to 30 September; rest of
the year, weekends and Wednesday
afternoons.
Local life, history and costume.

## Hambye Abbaye
Closed Tuesday and September to
March.
Marvellous ruined Romanesque and
Gothic abbey by River Sienne. Frescoes,
lapidary, period kitchen, Rouen
tapestries, all in restored Chapter
House.

## St Lô
Musée des Beaux-Arts
Open: daily 1 July to 31 August, daily;
rest of the year, afternoons.
Sixteenth-century tapestries, nineteenth-
century paintings.

Haras (Stud), full complement of
stallions present from 15 July to 15
February.

## Ste Marie-du-Mont
Musée du Débarquement
Open: Easter to 1 November, otherwise
weekends only.

Weapons, films, dioramas of the
Landings.

## Ste Mère-Église
Musée des Troupes Aeroportées
Open: all year.
Excellent military museum under
parachute-domed roof; photographs,
weapons, models, documents, 'Waco'
glider. First 'Liberty Way' marker stone
by Town Hall.

## Mont-St-Michel
Musée Historique, in 3 parts
Open: 21 March to 31 October.
Museums and audio-visual material,
waxworks, photographs, clocks —
history and life of Mount. One ticket
covers all three museums.

Abbaye du Mont-St-Michel
Open: all year.

## St Sauveur-le-Vicomte
Musée de Barbey d'Aurevilly
Open: July and August.
Displays on life and work of this writer
in his home town.

## Torigni-sur-Vire
Sixteenth-century Matignon Château
Open: 1 April to 15 September.
Period furniture and tapestries, shady
park, boating lake, walks.

## Valognes
Musée Regional du Cidre
Open: 15 June to 1 October except
Sunday mornings and holidays.
Cider-making in medieval buildings.

## Villedieu-les-Poëles
Fonderie des Cloches
Open: 1 May to 15 September, daily;
closed winter weekends.
Church bells cast in one of world's few
remaining bell foundries.

Copperware and Stove-making museum
Open: 1 June to 15 September.
Old workshop and exhibition of ware.

**Parc Zoologique de Champrepus**
8km west of Villedieu
Open: 1 March to 30 November.
Eighty species of animals and birds in
semi-freedom; refreshments and
souvenirs.

Furniture Museum
Open: 15 June to 15 September, daily;
Easter to June, Sundays and holidays.
Furniture from Rouen and Vire regions.

# Bibliography

Ardagh, John, *France in the 80's* (Penguin, 1982). Authoritative, in-depth examination of French society.

Collins, Martin, *The Visitor's Guide to the French Coast* (Moorland Publishing, 1985). Detailed tourist and background guide to coastline and resorts.

*Shell Guide to France* (Michael Joseph, 1985). Comprehensive gazetteer.

Neillands, Robin, *Guide to Normandy* (Robert Nicholson Publications, 1985). Pocket-sized gazetteer listing main towns and sights.

*Baedeker's France* (AA, Jarrold and Baedeker, Stuttgart, 1984). Background gazetteer.

Owen, Charles, *Just across the Channel* (Cadogan Books, 1983). Guide to day-trips and short holidays in northern France.

*Michelin Green Guide to Normandy*

Nicolson, Adam, *Long walks in France* (Weidenfeld and Nicolson Ltd 1983). Experiences and impressions on walks through French countryside.

# Index

149

# THE VISITOR'S GUIDE SERIES